The Future Has an Ancient Heart

Southern Italian Food Traditions in a Modern World

Nicole Kilburn

With Tonio Creanza
Photographs by Scott Cutler

The Future Has an Ancient Heart; Southern Italian Food Traditions in a Modern World

Published by Gusto Press
1180 Palmer Road
Victoria, British Columbia Canada
V8P 2H6

Library and Archives Canada Cataloguing in Publication information is available upon request.

ISBN: 978-1-9994662-0-6

CONTENTS

Acknowledgements

This book could not have been completed without the contributions and support of an incredible group of people. My thanks to Camosun College for supporting the research and writing, this experience has enriched me professionally beyond measure! In Italy, I am so grateful to the friendship and knowledge sharing, in particular Rosanna Denora (and her delicious food and infectious laugh), and Giovanni Maino and his family who generously included me in their Sunday at the farm. Countless others answered questions and put up with the endless curiosity of the anthropologist. Thank you to the Messors culinary workshop participants in 2015 and 2016 who helped me think about food based tourism from an insider's perspective, I hope that this book brings back memories of our many shared adventures. A special thank you to my friends Julie Marr and Francesco Creanza (and Janaki Larsen in 2016), part of the crack workshop team who helped make the magic happen and made it fun to work on 4 hours of sleep a night. Julie and Francesco, your help calibrating the recipes for a North American audience was essential, and a fun way to taste our memories at home in Victoria. Francesco, your insights, friendship and thoughtful conversations throughout the course of this project have made this book better- thank you!

The seeds of this book were planted by Tonio Creanza, which is appropriate since Messors is the Roman goddess of the harvest. Like any good farmer you have tended this crop through feedback and stimulating conversations, and are part of the finished product. It has been fascinating working with you.

My colleagues at Camosun College have offered expertise and support throughout this entire process. Thank you to David Blundon and Anna Collangelli in the biology department who helped to identify the plants collected in Giovanni's pasture. Joseph Ho's contributions with Photoshop and Illustrator helped create the cover. Tara Tudor and Katie Waterhouse have encouraged me along and provided invaluable anthropological perspectives along the way, not to mention friendship. Writing this book has benefited from the early feedback and editing of Julie Brennan (who also helped cook and photograph many of the recipes), and the incredible technical editing of Dale Mosher. Thank you for your tireless attention to detail, interest in the project, and friendship from Pugliese wheat fields to Oak Bay.

Thank you Scott for being my biggest supporter, for holding down the fort while I travelled to do this "grueling" research involving great food and wine and beautiful places, and for your beautiful photographs from our shared adventures in southern Italy in 2014. Thank you to my family, my children Alex and Olivia for their patience and my parents and parents-in-law for love and childcare help while I was in Italy.

This book is truly written on the backs of giants. I am very grateful.

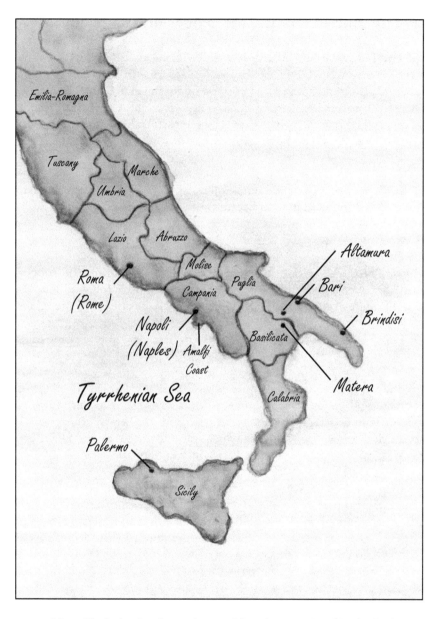

Map of Italy showing the provinces and key places mentioned in this book.

Timeline of cultural influences on Italy's south

Southern Italy is called *Mezzogiorno*, literally meaning "midday." In the traditional mariner language, *mezzogiorno* is the name of the wind from the south, and also coincides with the position of the sun at midday. Throughout its lengthy history, *Mezzogiorno* seemed to be a pawn in an unending series of conflicts and conquests by outsiders. The Greeks, Arabs, Normans, French, and Spanish all left their mark on the cuisine of southern Italy.

750 BC: The Greeks established a colony at Cumae (near Napoli). Many other colonies followed in what became known as *Magna Graecia*.

312 BC: The Via Appia was begun by Appius Claudius Caecus.

272 BC: The Greek colony of Tarentum surrendered to Roma and soon all remaining Greek colonies of the southern Italian peninsula followed suit. The Roman Empire exerted its political and cultural clout for many centuries.

AD 405: The development of the Eastern Roman Empire, centred in Constantinople (Byzantium).

After the fall of Rome (mid-400s) and the Gothic War (which ended in AD 554), the south was dominated by the Byzantines. As a result, much of southern Italy was aligned with Eastern religion, as seen by the spread of Eastern churches and monasteries which transmitted Greek and Hellenistic traditions (the foundation of shared Byzantine culture).

Following the Gothic War in the 6th century the Lombards (a Germanic group) annexed part of Calabria (along with much of northern Italy), and ruled the south until the 11th century when the Normans arrived. However, from the 9th century to the 11th century, the southern Italian peninsula was politically unstable and conflicts were epidemic.

AD 825: The Arabs arrived in Sicily, setting up several Islamic states, including the Emirate of Sicily and the Emirate of Bari. They brought new ingredients and food traditions. Rice arrived about AD 800 along with other new ingredients, or re-imagined existing ones.

AD 1071: The Normans from northern France conquered southern Italy.

AD 1198: The Normans were replaced by the Swabians, hailing from Germany. Frederick II built the Altamura Cathedral, amongst other structures.

AD 1264: Charles, of the house of Anjou, brother of French king Louis IX, unseated the Swabians, ending German rule. The German empire declined and the French asserted primacy over Europe. These were unsettling times. The next several centuries offered a dizzying jockeying for control of the south by other powerful western European royal families.

AD 1282: The (Spanish) Crown of Aragon invaded and supported a Sicilian rebellion against the French, which led to the War of the Sicilian Vespers. The outcome of this conflict was the division of the old Kingdom of Sicily in two (in 1302) whereby the island of Sicily went to the house of Aragon and the southern peninsula went to the house of Anjou. Spanish and French royal houses continued to fight over the southern Italian peninsula for centuries.

AD 1442: Alfonso V, King of Aragon, conquered the Kingdom of Naples and unified Sicily and Napoli once again as dependencies of the Crown of Aragon. This made the south more decidedly under Spanish rule, although the turmoil and competition between France and Spain continued for quite a while. Because southern Italy became part of the Crown of Spain, it was influenced earlier and more profoundly by many of the new foods from the Americas than were other parts of Europe.

Alfonso V established the *Dogana della Mene delle Pecore* ("Custom of the Sheep") to levy taxes on sheep and other livestock. The *Dogana* reduced the number of small farmers and agricultural labourers in southern Italy by favouring the conversion of cropland to pasture. The tension between farmer and shepherd is a long-standing one.

The House of Bourbon, a royal house of French origin, reigned over the Kingdom of Naples from the late 1700s until Italian unification in 1861. (This truly highlights how European royalty was bound together--the Bourbons had both a Spanish and a French branch.)

AD 1799: Napoleon Bonaparte captured Napoli and proclaimed it a French client state. The Bourbon king fled to Sicily.

AD 1815: The Bourbon king was reinstated to the throne following Napoleon's defeat. Unrest and rebellion were everyday fare in the decades leading up to Unification.

AD 1861: The political and social movement led by northerner Giuseppe Garibaldi culminated in the consolidation of the different states of the Italian peninsula into the single state of the Kingdom of Italy. The northern kingdom of Savoy, bolstered by the support of the Papal state, invaded the southern Kingdom of Bourbon. Florentine Italian was made the official Italian language, and even today prominent politicians tend to come from the north.

The economic gap between north and south was significant at the time of Unification. Road, rail and river transportation in the south was a fraction of the north, and concentrated near Napoli. Illiteracy in the south was about 87 percent, much higher than in the northern Piedmont at 54 percent. While the north embraced the development of capitalism and industry, the south languished. The south suffered from a legacy of centuries of foreign domination and neglect by distant rulers which really contributed to its poverty and isolation. It is not surprising that more than eighty percent of Italian immigrants who arrived in North America between 1880 and 1920 came from the south.

Today, the south remains less economically developed than the north and central regions, which benefited from the "economic miracle" in the 1950s and 1960s and became highly industrialized. This miracle was not realized to the same extent in the south, and many argue that the land reform policies of the 1950s resulted in the south becoming more and more dependent on state subsidies. A report published in July 2015 by the Italian organization SVIMEZ shows that Southern Italy had a negative GDP in the last seven years and that from the year 2000 it has been growing half as much as that of Greece.

1. Introduction

My introduction to Italy in 2014 was unconventional. First impressions were not of iconic Roman ruins, experienced in a crush of foreigners in key tourist hotspots. To be fair, Rome has been managing tourists for centuries and seems fairly well equipped to take it in stride. At the end of my first trip to Italy I spent a short time in Rome. A few days of seeing Roman ruins amid crowds of foreigners, and watching tourists pay for their photograph with men dressed as Roman centurions in front of the Coliseum was enough. It felt a bit choreographed and staged, and very different from the rest of my trip, which had been spent in the south. My first tastes of Italy included aged *ricotta forte* (an acquired taste), horsemeat in tomato sauce, and homemade *limoncello digestif*. This introduction was guided by Tonio Creanza, a native of Altamura in the southern province of Puglia (and collaborator on this book), whose company--Messors--and culinary workshops are a different brand of tourism. Tonio's itinerary, which showcases the landscape that his family has lived in for at least the last five generations, is not what you would read about in a Lonely Planet guidebook. For example, the first time I visited Matera, a cave settlement that is one of the oldest continuously occupied towns on Earth, Tonio asked if anyone wanted to walk up to an exceptional viewpoint. Many preferred to sit in the shade with a beer, but a few of us were game. What followed was an adventurous scramble up an outcrop of hard limestone, which included a ten-foot vertical climb up a rock face that attracted the amused attention of locals. We got to the top, breathless, and were rewarded with an astonishing view of the cave neighbourhoods (called *sassi*) laid out along the edge of the ravine and our friends sitting far below in the Piazza San Pietro Caveoso. Tonio has been climbing up this rock since he was a child, and this was just one example of getting to experience this landscape like a local, a backstage pass that often is not available to tourists.

This got me thinking about some of the key differences between my first impressions of southern Italy and the mainstream tourism economy. Messors offers a very different style of tourism, and its philosophy about heritage and tapping tourism as a form of constructive economic and social development inspired this book. I would define my experience as an exclusive one; I was invited to walk alongside a local with a contagious passion for his home, and experience authentic interactions with locals, something that can be hard to do as a tourist. Tonio and his family have lived and worked and dreamed in this landscape, and have been shaped by the Murgia Plateau in much the same way that climate and soil acidity impart a taste to the food of

1

that place. We foraged for wild asparagus and rocket in farmers' fields that we then cooked into frittata for dinner. We bought produce in the street market and were serenaded by a vendor who sang opera to make us laugh. At the Bari fish market we sipped ice-cold Peroni beer alongside fishermen, which paired perfectly with the fresh raw seafood over which we squeezed lemon wedges and ate as a mid-morning snack. We met a shepherd and made cheese from his sheep's milk. I visited nuns in a cloistered nunnery in Scala, a small town that hugs the steep slopes that sweep down to the Amalfi Coast. They served us lemon shaved ice and sent us on our way with smiles, kisses, and a box of lemon biscotti. It was incredible, and I appreciated the profound connections to this landscape that can still be tasted in the food and the cultural traditions that have been shaped by it for thousands of years.

This initial experience made me curious about not only the food traditions that I was being exposed to, but also how the embrace of tourism (and specifically heritage tourism with a focus on food) affects the vitality of these traditions in a modern world. I realized that Messors was not a typical tourism venture, and I became interested in how tourism can become part of sustainable economic development in a region grappling with the challenges of high unemployment and limited economic opportunity. In 2015 and 2016 I worked with Tonio to help facilitate the workshop I first participated in, using my background as an anthropologist to not only help participants think about the food traditions of southern Italy, but also to study the dynamics of tourism from an insider's perspective. This book is a reflection of the rich food traditions I have encountered, and a critical evaluation of food-based tourism and heritage designations that can both validate and tarnish them.

If you get lost in romantic visions of rolling green landscapes, ruins, and weathered-looking farmers and shepherds when you try to imagine southern Italy, you will be happy to know that your daydreams can be pretty accurate. It is a stunning landscape, and complex food traditions can be found at every turn. But this book is not going to tell fanciful stories that make you think you are going to step back in time when you visit southern Italy. The intention here is not to offer descriptions of idyllic, timeless rural Italian cuisine, beautifully and mercifully untouched by the fast-paced and often ugly elements of the industrialized world. A world in a bubble does not exist, not even in the wheat fields of Puglia, where the silence can hurt a city dweller's ears when they first arrive, and the darkness at night is so absolute that it is disorienting. This book is about food traditions in the modern south, and explores how meaningful elements of culture, whose foundations stretch back centuries, fit into a modern, globalized world (or don't). Why are these foodways important to the people that engage with them, from the producers to ultimate consumers, including a growing number of tourists looking for an "authentic" Italian travel experience? What common themes lead to their vulnerabilities, and how are they being redefined to stay vital?

Balancing heritage and modernity can be tricky; in tourism the demands of visitors can shape the expressions of heritage that they travel to experience. There is also a risk that the valuation of "traditional foods" stagnates these expressions of culture, expecting them to be unchanged in ingredients and preparation since time immemorial. What becomes obvious in the various foods considered in this book is that they all have dynamic pasts, and our definition of "tradition" must be flexible enough to accommodate this while honouring the cultural importance of these foods.

Connection and disconnect

Food tourism is a niche market that is experiencing huge growth. This popularity is likely driven by a number of things, maybe the same things that are behind the recent farm-to-table movements that have swept North America and their vocal interest in and support of local food producers. The growing interest in food in North America comes at a time when our food system is experiencing huge change. Our food landscape would have been almost unrecognizable to our great-grandparents; imagine them stumbling into a large grocery store, blinded by the fluorescent lights and stunned by the seemingly endless aisles of processed food stretching off into the distance. A century ago half of all families in North America lived in rural landscapes or small towns of less than 2,500 inhabitants. There was more geographic connection to food because more food was grown locally instead of being imported from far afield; fruits like bananas had made their appearance but they were rare and seasonal, and expensive. Even my grandmother, who grew up in Ontario, Canada, remembers oranges as a special treat around Christmas; she once commented on a moldy orange in my fruit bowl, saying that as a child oranges were so special that they were **never** wasted by getting old!

Our increasingly industrialized reality challenges our connections to food production, the environment, and one another. As more and more humans find themselves living in urban environments (and in 2008 we passed a significant milestone when over half of our species now live in urban contexts), it is easy to forget about our essential connection to the land, which is so clearly presented by the food we eat. We forget that foods have seasons, that producing food takes great effort and knowledge, and that aspects of the landscape in which a food is produced can *actually* be tasted in the food itself. Consumers may know very little about where their food comes from, who grows it and how, and the compromises of the industrial food system where quantity and profitability are prized over taste. These seem to represent great disconnects, yet the connections between consumers and producers, and between humans and their landscapes are vital--we forget them at our peril. Many industrialized eaters have forgotten the taste of fresh, in-season produce bred for flavour rather than yield. In the din of our very busy lives we do not necessarily see what has been muted and deprioritized. But in "getting away from it all" on vacation, a tourist may catch a glimpse of these sacrifices. Stepping off the treadmill of life, one can reconnect with important things like time spent with family, good food, and good company. These can be some of the most enjoyable parts of being on holiday, and can make returning to "the real world" a bit of a hard landing. This quest to reconnect, in a variety of different ways, is likely another key driver in the rising popularity of food and agriculturally-based tourism.

When food is reduced to fuel, to calories and macronutrients, the great stories of our food are forgotten, and homogenization, a watchword of industrialism, sets in. The McDonald's slogan "One Taste Worldwide" rather sums up this modern human eating; National Geographic research has tracked changes in diets around the world over the past five decades, and highlights a clear trend towards homogenization. Increasingly, we are eating the same things, which is a reflection of the influence of globalization and the complex socio-economics of the industrial food system. With 50,000 edible plants to choose from, the Federal Agricultural Organization (FAO) reports that the majority of humans now derive the majority of their calories from just fifteen crops. This might make sense when you are talking about efficiency and profits, but as omnivores we are not designed for this kind of homogenization. It is problematic to our bodily health, and our diverse cultural spirits. To those who are not interested in living in a monochromatic world, it is time to act. As a wise French saying reminds us: *"People only eat to live when they do not understand how to live to eat."* In being disconnected in myriad ways we have forgotten how to do this.

The future has an ancient heart

The title of this book is a call to arms. When Carlo Levi, a political activist, artist and writer said this in 1956, he was not referring to food. (If he had been, he might have said stomach.) He was talking about more than just food, more than just one element of culture--he was referring to the whole thing, the rich, complex web of culture that makes people who they are. In the 1950s, as the horrors of WWII began to recede and Italy embraced modernity as it rebuilt itself, all gazes were firmly set on the future. The past, it seemed, was one of misery, and darkness, and hunger, especially in the poor southern regions of Italy, a rural landscape of peasants and shepherds impoverished by centuries of largess by absentee landlords and foreign interests. This was epitomized in towns like Matera, where dirty children

4

lounged in the streets and families shared caves with donkeys and other livestock, where malaria and cholera were everyone's neighbours in the cave *sassi*. This "National Shame" was a blemish on the fresh promises of the future, and there was extreme pressure to cast off tradition and replace it with a clean, sanitized, modern identity. But Levi, despite having lived alongside the citizens of Basilicata during the war, having heard children crying in the night from bellies knotted in hunger, still counseled that a vibrant future depends on maintaining the critical elements of heritage. Expressions of heritage are the essential organs of a living culture; if the heart stops beating, the soul is gone. A key expression of this heritage, this sense of rootedness and identity, is food. Modernity has certainly embraced homogenization, but what is at stake? When traditional foodways fade, a whole cultural and environmental complex risks being lost. The accumulated gastronomic brilliance that has won food from challenging landscapes and absorbed the ingredients from a revolving door of outside influences to become part of regional identities is under threat. The loss of a food's flavour is an obvious forfeiture, but this is really the tip of the iceberg. What may be harder to see and appreciate is the loss of knowledge to produce these foods, knowledge accumulated over generations. More broadly, there is the loss of rural livelihoods and, in the case of rural depopulation, the loss of entire communities and the way of life found there. There is also the real risk of losing the working landscapes that have produced these foods and given them their special *terroir*, and the withering of biodiversity as the focus shifts to efficiency and maximum yield. Matera is the epitome of this disconnect, a sobering reminder that when people become disconnected from their landscape, decline and decay are inevitable. Matera offers a cautionary tale about the hazards of unsustainable relationships with the landscape, and a model for modern reinvention and cultural revitalization. As we look to the future, cultural traditions must play key roles in the modern world. Culinary tourism has the potential to offer sustainable economic development that satisfies the interests of travelers wanting to reconnect with these elements, and of locals trying to maintain their connection to them.

Re-learning how to "live to eat" means re-establishing connections

Food is an excellent way to think about connections, and this book explores many of them. Food can be a connection to complex histories and disparate geographies. Food is a visible expression of identity, represents the essential connection between humans and their landscape, and can be used to connect us to other human beings in the past, the present and into the future. The food on our plates offers fascinating history lessons. Flavours are reminders of conquest, tragedy, and resilience. Olive oil, a unifying item of the Mediterranean diet that transcends ethnic groups, religion, and geography, is a legacy of Phoenician traders who spread olive trees throughout the Mediterranean basin thousands of years ago. Many ingredients that are hallmarks of Italian cuisine today reflect the influence of foreigners. Tomatoes, for example, were brought to southern Italy by the Spanish in the 1500s, who had encountered these fruits as they explored the Americas and then brought them back to Europe. The presence of Arabs in Italy's south is remembered through the widespread use of lemons and almonds; Arabs were also the likely donors of noodles, which they had encountered in Asia, and in Italy they became the basis of pasta. These histories are explored in the short photo essays of this book.

New understandings of food also come from making direct connections to the producers themselves. The industrial food system is supported by faceless producers, whom consumers are often separated from both geographically and psychologically. This disconnect is one of the reasons why deplorable working conditions can persist in food production such as Puglia's tomato industry; consumers choosing a jar of tomato sauce in a grocery store make decisions based on price, driving the pay of agricultural labourers down as companies strive to compete. They can't see the long days, the low wages, the sub-standard living conditions that are invisible ingredients in the jar. When you spend time with the people who produce your food, and have the opportunity to learn about their craft, the awareness adds another dimension to the food. When you think about the baker, who starts work in the middle of the night because the rhythm of his day is dictated by the rising of the dough more than his watch, you begin to understand that his bread is not just his job but his way of life. Being introduced to the daily and seasonal rhythms of a shepherd is similar; every day is structured by the animals' need to graze in pastures, regardless of whether they are producing milk that can be sold. This demonstrates the care and investment that goes into a flock every day for the promise of food that is produced for less than half the year. Being reminded of these realities helps reconnect us with food and think about its production and consumption in new ways.

Terroir: Tasting the connection to place

When items seem to miraculously appear on store shelves, the consumer can also be unaware of the heartbeats of the landscape. Food generally represents the seasonal rhythms of a place. This means eating foods when they are in season, like wild chicory and asparagus foraged from the fields. But it also relates to the variations in how a food will taste, called *terroir*. What the sheep eat in the early spring is different from what they eat in the dry days of mid-summer when herbs have finished blooming and the landscape looks brown and parched. These variations affect the flavours of their milk, which in turn produces cheeses that taste different. *Terroir* is the opposite of homogenization; it is a celebration of diversity that comes from producers working with the variations of time and space instead of exerting absolute control so that a product can be the same every single time a consumer purchases it. It introduces something of a wild card, an uncertainty which is often something to avoid at all costs in the context of business. But when a food producer relinquishes total control and lets the landscape have a hand in shaping the final product, magical, delicious things can happen. Cheeses aged in caves reflect the variation that can come from naturally present yeasts, temperature fluctuations, breezes, and humidity, all of which contribute to the flavour of the cheese. Like a child raised with the values of its family, a food aged this way matures as a product of its landscape.

I believe *terroir* is more than the mineral composition of the soils in which food is grown, or the amount of rainfall or sunlight that a particular bunch of grapes or lemon receives. The intangible contributors, like the passion of food producers, the care they demonstrate, the dedication to doing things the way their parents did, and the pride in sharing their products with others all seem to make their way into the finished products. And the consumer offers something too: how many times have you thought that a meal you cooked was exceptional because of the effort *you* put into acquiring the ingredients, and the care you put into making it? Some would say you are tasting the love in the food--simplistic perhaps. But you can only distinguish these components when you are an active part of the equation and can appreciate those connections to people and place.

The desire to make these connections is a key element of food-based tourism and the quest for authentic travel experiences. What I have learned from Messors' approach to facilitating these connections has become the foundation of this book: to understand the food you have to understand the culture. To understand the culture you have to understand the landscape. With this integrated, holistic approach, food becomes a lens to appreciate history, social relationships, human ecology, tradition, and identity. It places consumers as key participants instead of passive end-users. Eating the food, you cannot help but contemplate the broader contexts, and as you explore the region, be it physically or as a reader, you start to think about the food on your plate in new ways. Becoming an active participant is empowering. When visitors appreciate the knowledge of food producers and engage in the experience instead of just passively moving through the space, they are activists fighting to protect these critical, living aspects of culture.

Setting the Stage: The human-landscape connection of the Murgia Plateau

The landscape is a great shaper of the human condition. Nowhere is this more evident than in the southern regions of Puglia and Basilicata. The south is dominated by the Apennine mountains, which run down the peninsula like a spine and make much of the land too steep to farm. This entire landscape was once covered by the sea, and millennia of deposition on the sea bottom created the fossil-embossed limestone that is now the Murgia Plateau. This is a dry environment; annual rainfall rarely exceeds 510 mm (20 inches) and comes in torrential downpours during the winter and spring. Surface water is rare since water quickly penetrates the limestone, and groundwater can be extremely deep (in some areas you have to drill 800 meters to find the water table!). Water is precious and expensive. There is a lengthy tradition of capturing rainwater during the wet season in giant cisterns for use at drier times of the year, an ethic of sustainability represented quite strikingly in places like Matera that the modern world could stand to learn from. The scarcity of water has shaped food production in the region; food producers have focused on crops that are more drought resistant, like almonds and olives, which are well suited to fending for themselves in hot, un-irrigated environments (at the expense of yield). Even the variety of sheep traditionally kept on the Murgia Plateau--the *Altamurana* breed--are adapted to these marginal conditions.

The geology of the Murgia Plateau has undeniably shaped the way the landscape has been used for thousands of years. The rocky limestone hills that are not well suited for farming have been used by shepherds, whose flocks of sheep and goats convert wild grasses and fragrant herbs into milk, meat, and wool, which historically were key elements of the region's economy. The pockets of more fertile land have been used for small farmers' fields; rather than a sea of mono-cropping stretching out over the horizon, the landscape is a patchwork of poly-culture, with wheat and grapes and olives and almonds, and a host of other crops, growing shoulder to shoulder. This low intensity food production that weaves farmers and shepherds together on the same landscape doesn't generate huge yields, but has been a successful way to produce the ingredients of *la cucina povera* for thousands of years.

Humans have lived as part of this landscape for a very long time; a cave not far from Altamura is the last resting place for "Altamura Man," the remains of a Neanderthal who lived at least 70,000 years ago (2016 research suggests the remains may be 130,000 years old). The nearby city of Matera, hugging the rim of a plunging ravine, has caves excavated from the soft tufa limestone that have been in use for the last 9,000 years. The Greeks have come and gone, and the Roman Empire too, but the complementary blending of farm and shepherding has persisted, taking on the influences that come with new people and ideas and making them part of the Murgia Plateau.

Historically, the landscape has influenced the art, food, culture, and architecture because it offers the basic materials for building, and the type of soil for cultivation. It also seems to have influenced the hyper-regionalism of food and culture; every town has its own special dishes, variations on the local theme. *La cucina povera*--literally "poverty food"--is not fairly translated into English. It describes the art of frugal cooking, and is not patronizing in considering this simple yet delicious food. It is comprised of basic ingredients local to the area, and not burdened with foreign spices. It is a rural peasant cuisine that reflects thrift, making the most of what the land will provide: pasta made without eggs, bread wrested from the hard-grain durum wheat of the Murgia Plateau, and the use of many wild vegetables (like *cicorielle*, wild chicory, and *lampascioni*, the bulb of a wild tassel hyacinth) and flavours (like wild fennel and thyme). Although *la dolce vita* defies being reduced into isolated parts, North Americans have become enamored by the food component--the so-called "Mediterranean diet"--and its association with good health and longevity. This millennia old heritage shared by populations of the Mediterranean has been linked to lower incidence of heart disease and possibly to decreased rates of some cancers and Alzheimer's disease. What North Americans can miss with this approach is that the diet is more than just the food; it cannot be replicated simply by eating mostly vegetables, fruits, grains, legumes, nuts, and olive oil, all washed down with a daily glass of red wine. "Diet," from the Greek word *dia-ita*, means "way of living" or "lifestyle," and incorporates not just what is eaten, but how it is eaten. Reconnecting with food, people, and landscape takes time and explicit effort, and these ingredients are just as important in realizing the health benefits as the olive oil and red wine. In recognition of the complexity and importance of the Mediterranean diet, it was inscribed into UNESCO's list of intangible cultural heritage of humanity in 2013. In doing so, the UN identifies this living heritage as the source of humanity's cultural diversity, the protection of which is essential for continued creativity. *"This intangible cultural heritage, transmitted from generation to generation, is constantly recreated by communities and groups in response to their environment, their interaction with nature and their history, and provides them with a sense of identity and continuity, thus promoting respect for cultural diversity and human creativity."*

This living heritage embodied in diet is obvious in Altamura, the town in Puglia that is at the geographic epicentre of this book. Locals collect wild edibles and eat foods grown themselves or by neighbours and family members. Their menus change seasonally, which introduces great variety to one's meals. The community is still very connected to its food and food traditions, in part because the relationships between producers and consumers are still fairly close ones. Most people know food producers, or are producers themselves; it is still common to buy wine from friends who have vats of good homemade table wine in their small basements, or to source food directly from where it is grown or made. Children can still recognize a host of vegetables by name because they see them grown and cooked and placed on the family table to share. This makes it a great place to learn about food traditions, and learn about the value of food traditions in a rapidly changing world. As Claude Levi Strauss said, *"Food has to be not only good to eat but good to think."* The hidden histories, identities, and social values of southern Italian food seem to hit the mark on both fronts.

2. In the *Masseria* kitchen

To begin to understand the connection between humans, food traditions, and the landscape in southern Italy, one must be introduced to some key elements of architecture. Each is important on their own, but taken together, reveal a complex set of interrelationships that have existed for centuries, with roots that extend back even further. These buildings have housed the people who have crafted the food traditions we appreciate today.

Historically, the countryside of the south was divided into expansive estates owned by absentee landlords. This set up a feudal-style system whereby aristocrats lived in opulence in urban centres like Napoli or regional centres like Altamura and Gravina, while their land was worked by tenant food producers and seasonal labourers. These large, diverse estates were called *latifondi*, and located at their heart, both geographically and administratively, was a *masseria* (farmhouse). The *masseria* was technically the residence of the landowner, but since these absentee landlords rarely visited their holdings, the *masseria* was the temporary residence for the agent and the estate manager, who negotiated the land leases, hired the field hands, and collected rent from tenants. Sometimes tenants would live in quarters that formed part of the *masseria* compound, and seasonal workers would also be housed there in cramped quarters for the duration of the harvest. The *masseria's* architecture, with the landlord's living rooms surrounded by smaller quarters for personnel, stores, and stables, and a chapel for all who were affiliated with this landscape, reflected the hierarchical pattern of the estates.

Masseria Jesce, a 16ᵗʰ century fortified farmhouse on the Appian Way just outside Altamura. The open area in the front was used by peasants for communal processing activities such as wool production.

Masseria la Selva ("*farmhouse in the woods*") is a bit different from other *masserie* in the region because it actually started as a hunting lodge. Built in the 1780s for the Gravina line of the powerful Orsini family, members of the nobility would use the lodge when they hunted fox and boar in the oak forests, much of which has now been cleared for farmland. A semi-circular, walled enclosure at the front of the building was originally meant to contain the hunting dogs. The Lorusso family, who bought the original 400-hectare property when the Orsinis declared bankruptcy in 1917, maintain it as a working farm; historically it grew tobacco, and the addition of barns on either side were for drying tobacco and housing the 150-200 labourers that lived in the barns of the *masseria* during the few weeks of the harvest. Today the fields grow durum wheat, barley, cotton, and fava beans. There are sheep and cows, and an assortment of farm dogs and cats. A hired shepherd lives in part of the *masseria* near the stables and looks after the animals that are part of the cheese-making operation that takes place in a low building on the left side of the *masseria*'s compound.

La Selva's farm is typical of small-scale farming in Puglia. Low intensity shepherding and farming practices have developed together to meet the environmental constraints of the region. While fertile areas are the domain

An abandoned jazzo returns to the rocky soils of the Murgia Plateau.

of small groves of olives, almonds, pears, grapevines, and fields of wheat and fava beans, the rockier areas, where the soils are quite poor, are used by the shepherds. Traditionally, shepherds used complexes called *jazzi* (pronounced yatsi), their spartan living space away from their family homes in town. Like tenant farmers who leased farmland on these estates, shepherds would rent the *jazzo*, designed first and foremost for the animals. Long, rectangular, stone enclosures to contain the shepherd's sheep and goats were built on a slope to make it easier to wash out the stalls. Terraces acted like gutters, slowing the movement of surface water so that it could be collected in cisterns. In addition to shelter for the animals, *jazzi* have space for milking, and a cheese-making room called a *casone*. Only rarely would the shepherd have separate living space, instead placing a bed in the *casone* as needed. Shepherding products were produced in the countryside and then brought to markets in town.

Shepherds also used caves carved from the layers of soft limestone that are exposed across much of the landscape they traversed with their animals. Caves are common around Altamura, Gravina, and Matera where the soft tufa yields easily to both natural elements and human effort. The Fornello cave site demonstrates the multiple uses of caves over time. The site dates from the

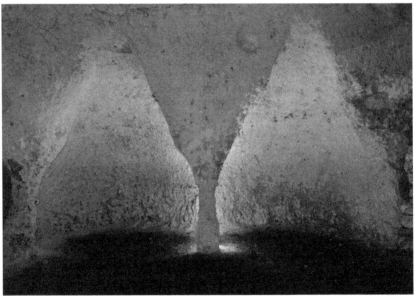

A cave entrance gapes out of the side of a limestone hill at the Fornello site. Inside, small excavated areas may have been stalls for animals; water troughs are carved out of the nearby tufa walls. However, these may originally have been small cells for Byzantine monks who occupied the site in the 12ᵗʰ and 13ᵗʰ centuries. It is hard to know without excavation.

3rd century BC, and was used by Byzantine monks in the 12th century who left frescos in a cave church. These caves were reinvented once again for use by shepherds and their animals when they needed shelter.

Trulli are another distinctive form of architecture in Puglia, dry-stacked conical structures that historically served as field houses for farmers and (less so) shepherds. This form of architecture is truly a product of its landscape.

People say that *"this land grows stone"* because it is constantly coming up from below a shallow layer of topsoil. Farmers tirelessly clear their fields, so there is a lot of building material. Additional stone would come from excavating the cistern, the first job when setting up a farmstead in a landscape with no surface water and very dry summers. The limestone excavated from these water storage features came out like thick books rather than carved tufa blocks, making them perfect for the dry-stack spiral construction of *trulli*. Stories abound of *trulli* being made without mortar so that they could be easily made uninhabitable by removing the top (and thus letting the rain in) and therefore avoiding visits from the tax collector, but this is likely more of a story than reality. The more functional--but less exciting--explanation is that there is no surface water in southern Puglia, so sand imported for mortar would have been expensive.

The table is set for lunch in front of a restored trullo near Ceglie Mesappica.

Trulli architecture can be traced back to the 1660s, although it may be much older. The construction is very simple, and the building material has always been abundant; at one time everyone in the countryside in the Valle d'Itria lived like this. After World War II modernity cast the countryside as a poor landscape, and over the decades more and more people have either moved away entirely or moved into town, changing the relationship between humans and their landscape and the dynamics between town and country. Many *trulli* sit abandoned and crumbling amongst centuries old olive trees. More recently, interest has been revived through tourism, and in 1996 this architectural style was included in the UNESCO list of World Heritage Sites. Since then *trulli* have become icons of Puglia; many have been restored and turned into exotic vacation rentals or hotels to capitalize on their unique appeal.

Taken together, the *masserie, jazzi, trulli,* and towns of Italy's south illustrate a complex interconnection between humans and their landscape. Food traditions have been customized to meet the challenges of the environment, and while the emphasis on various local products has shifted over the years, the absolute connection between them has stayed vital. The relationship between humans and this landscape has always been a dynamic one, but in the past sixty years the southern peninsula has witnessed huge change, encouraged by the drive for modernity following World War II. This change has included, and influenced, intensification of production, out-migration as big cities and the promise of employment entice youth away, and a growing disconnect that threatens the integrity of these traditions and places. What does the future hold? All of these modern woes can be forgotten for a time as you stand in the *masseria* kitchen and help Rosanna cook. Local, seasonal food such as brown mushrooms, fava beans, artichokes, and chicory sit in the cool dark pantry waiting to be transformed into a delicious meal prepared on the worn marble table in the centre of the room. A farm dog sits at the back door, looking in. Music fills the air. People come and go. The kitchen is truly the heart of the operation, and the food is its spirit.

A Meal from the *Masseria* Kitchen, from Rosanna Denora

This four-course meal uses seasonal and everyday ingredients for simple, delicious food that invokes the tastes of Puglia, and sharing an evening with friends. These recipes serve 6-8 adults.

Primo: *Orecchiette al forno con polpette, funghi e formaggio pecorino fresco*
(Baked pasta with meatballs, mushrooms and cheese)

To make the *sugo* (sauce) for both courses:

- 1 large onion, finely diced
- 2 large garlic cloves, minced
- 3 ~700ml jars of *passata di pomodori* (crushed tomatoes)
- 500g mushrooms (cardoncelli mushrooms would be used in Puglia in June, but button mushrooms are also delicious), sliced (dice the stems)
- Salt to taste (adding a pinch to the onions helps them sweat)
- Basil

Start by sautéing the onion in olive oil until soft and translucent, then add the minced garlic. Pour the *passata* into the pan and simmer.

Take a portion of the *sugo* and reserve for the parmigiana dish (secondo). Then add the mushrooms and basil into the larger portion of *sugo* and keep on a simmer.

For the *polpette* (meatballs):

- 2 pieces of bread
- 500g ground pork sausage
- 1 egg
- 1 clove of garlic, minced
- 2 ½ Tbsp. parsley, chopped
- Pinch of salt
- 150 g grated Pecorino cheese, for layering

Make fresh breadcrumbs by toasting the bread and pulverizing it with a rolling pin. Add to the ground pork sausage, along with the egg, garlic, parsley, and salt. Roll into small balls, about the size of a marble. Add the *polpette* to the *sugo* so that there is a good proportion of *polpette* and sauce (any extra *polpette* can be fried separately).

Cook 750 g of dried orecchiette pasta al dente. Pasta can be slightly undercooked since it will be baked in the oven.

Layer the *sugo* with *polpette* and pasta into a 9-inch square baking pan. Start with a layer of *sugo*, then pasta, then grated pecorino cheese. Continue with these layers until you get to the top of the pan or have used all the pasta and *sugo*. Put grated cheese on top (a pecorino cheese would be Rosanna's choice, but any hard cheese will be delicious), and drizzle olive oil on the top (Rosanna's secret). Bake at 375 degrees F. Check after 30 minutes. When the top is brown (about 40 minutes total cooking time) it's finished.

Secondo: *Parmigiana alla Rosanna*
(Baked eggplant with layers of meat and cheese)

- 2 large eggplants
- ½ cup flour (in southern Italy this would be hard durum wheat)
- 2 eggs, beaten
- 340g fresh mozzarella, broken into small pieces
- 200 g Prosciutto or mortadella, thinly sliced
- 50 g grated Parmigiano-Reggiano or pecorino cheese

Peel and slice the eggplants into long strips (about ¼ inch thick). Put them in water with a bit of salt, which removes the vegetable's bitterness and some of the tough texture if the eggplant is a bit older. Weight down the slices with something heavy on top of a plate (in a colander), for 30 minutes. Then rinse the slices and dry them very well. Dry-grill the eggplant in a hot, cast iron skillet so that the eggplant doesn't soak up lots of oil.

In a 9-inch square baking pan, layer as follows:
sugo, fried eggplant, mozzarella, meat, *sugo*, etc. until the pan is full.

Top with *sugo*, grated cheese, and a bit of olive oil, and bake in a 375 degree F oven for 20 minutes.

Salad: *Carpaccio di zucchini*

The word *carpaccio* means a dish of raw ingredients, often raw meats or fish but in this case zucchini, that are sliced paper thin and served with a drizzle of something acidic (lemon or vinegar), olive oil, salt and pepper. The acid marinade breaks down the zucchini, in essence cooking it and giving it a softened texture. The process also allows the oil, mint and salt to penetrate and leave their tastes throughout the dish.

- 1-2 medium sized zucchini
- The juice from 2 medium lemons
- A large handful of fresh mint, chopped
- Extra virgin olive oil
- salt

Thinly slice the zucchini; a mandolin works very well for this. Lay out the pieces on a plate or shallow bowl, preferably one with a lip to accommodate the liquids.

Sprinkle the salt evenly over the zucchini, then spoon over the lemon juice, making sure to get good coverage.

Sprinkle the chopped mint on top, and add a generous drizzle of olive oil.

Dolce:

Fruit salad with *Limoncello*

Take a selection of seasonal fruits and dice into a bowl. Before serving add 1-2 Tbsp chopped mint, pour chilled limoncello (recipe p. 126) over the fruit and toss lightly.

Chocolate-covered Almonds

- 1 ½ cups whole almonds
- 1 ¾ cups semi-sweet chocolate chips or chopped pieces of chocolate
- 3 Tbsp almond flour

Place almonds on a cookie sheet and lightly toast in the oven. Once they have cooled, put a teaspoon of almonds into each small paper cupcake wrapper. In a microwave or double boiler, melt some dark chocolate, then spoon over each cluster of almonds. A light dusting of almond flour over the top is a nice decorative touch. Let cool for several hours before serving.

3. Imagining Italy: Culinary tourism and the construction of food identity

Close your eyes, and picture Italy...maybe a green rolling countryside with a villa perched on top of a hill comes to mind, the approach lined with tall, thin cypress trees, the air hazy in the hot afternoon light. Maybe there is a vineyard, a steaming plate of spaghetti, or an ancient shepherd moving his sheep across a pasture, or a loud gathering of people around a long dinner table that will feature fantastic food, wine, and laughter that stretches late into the evening. These images are shared by many prospective travelers because various forms of media, from movies and books, to the advertisements of travel companies, build a stereotyped narrative that creates expectations about what Italy will be like. Travelers make decisions based on these expectations, regardless of their validity: don't go to Napoli because it's dirty and crime riddled, live *la dolce vita* in Tuscany, check out the southern peninsula to experience a place that is stuck in time. Tourists choose to go somewhere based on their interests and how they envision spending their hard-earned leisure time. But the expectations that tourists bring with them have the power to shape what they actually experience, a stereotyped, and self-fulfilling prophesy instead of unexpected authenticity.

Destinations transformed by and for tourists can become less than pleasant places for residents to live, as they have to contend with crowds, increased cost of goods and services, and a degradation of the built environment. This tradeoff is particularly poignant as regions off the beaten tourist path in southern Italy seek economic and cultural salvation by embracing the tourism industry, and outcomes can leave a bitter taste in locals' mouths. How can tourism be shaped to meet the needs of *all* stakeholders? How can the expectations of tourists, with money to spend in communities that need it, be met while fulfilling the needs of locals, who gamble that heritage tourism, and specifically a focus on food heritage, will dignify and invigorate these traditions in a modern world? For tourism to be part of sustainable economic development, more than just hard economic indicators must be considered; a critical and honest evaluation of how culinary tourism can both validate and tarnish these traditions and places is required.

Tuscany, a leader in agritourism in Italy, and renowned as a culinary tourism destination is a region that until recently was better known for its poverty. This makes Tuscany a useful lens through which to consider

23

contemporary developments in culinary tourism in southern Italy where communities are trying to address similar social, cultural and economic challenges and are actively courting tourists. Although Puglia has been a vacation destination for northern Italians for some time, its fairly recent "discovery" by British and North American tourists is shaping the Tourist Rush that is sweeping the region. Billed as a quiet, untouched, rural paradise where people continue to live lives relatively untouched by the "modern world," the region is quickly becoming a top travel destination. This makes a critical evaluation of the costs and benefits of tourism very timely; the hope is that learning from other regions such as Tuscany may provide guidance on how to better balance the tourism equation in favour of local interests.

Italy has a lengthy history of immersive tourism. The Grand Tour, which arguably launched the modern western phenomenon of tourism in the mid 17th century, was a rite of passage for aristocrats from Britain and northern Europe, and Italy was a prime destination. Although it was not a scholarly pilgrimage, the objective was primarily educational; wealthy young men participated in "study abroad" to cultivate experiences that increased knowledge and created opportunities for studying new languages, culture and arts. Travel was considered an essential form of stimulus to develop the mind, the ultimate liberal education. In a time before photography and the Internet, the Grand Tour was the only way to see key works of art or hear particular music. Richard Lassels's *"Voyage of Italy"*, published in 1670, highlighted four elements of the Grand Tour that made it so important for young travelers: intellectual, social, and political development, and ethical self-improvement. As steam trains and ocean travel became more accessible to the middle class, beginning in the 1800s, the cache of the grand Tour waned, and tourism changed, in focus and objective.

Today, tourism is big business, and forms a significant part of Italy's economy. In 2015, foreign tourists spent almost 36 billion euros, and are coming in increasing numbers; notably, American visitors increased by 10% in that year over 2014 statistics. Tourism accounts for 11.8% of the national GDP and is directly responsible for 12.8% of jobs nationally. Like the Grand Tourists, who followed a fairly standard itinerary featuring places like Venice and Rome, until very recently, most of the forty million foreign tourists who visit Italy annually have concentrated their interest (and money) in these key destinations, and the beaches of northern Italy. Similar to the Grand Tourists, who made it to Napoli to see the ruined cities of Pompeii and Herculaneum, few ventured farther into southern Italy.

Under the broad umbrella of tourism, culinary tourism is experiencing huge growth globally; statistics from 2013 identify almost three-quarters of the US adult population as leisure travelers, people who have enjoyed at least one vacation in the past year, and 77% of *them* are classified as culinary travelers. A culinary tourist is someone whose itinerary is intentionally shaped by the desire to learn about the culinary traditions of a new place, to engage all of the senses, and be immersed in the experience. This niche market is an opportunity for Italy's less popular regions to attract tourists by commodifying the rural experience and traditional foodways.

Since the 1950s economists have argued that becoming part of the global market is an effective strategy for poverty reduction: modernize, experience higher levels of material wealth, and all will be well. This is a key motivation in rural tourism; communities struggling with the challenges of high unemployment and limited economic opportunity are throwing open their doors and welcoming the world. But to integrate into this global market you have to have something to sell--and someone who wants to buy it. Since the distinctiveness of place is key to attracting visitors to a destination, it is not surprising that regional foods have much to offer in terms of branding. Because they have to be experienced in context, regional foodways have distinctive tourist appeal and their representation in tourism has the potential to not only support local economies but also maintain local identity and biodiversity, all of which are beneficial to locals and should lead to positive tourism development for everyone. The growing interest in culinary tourism comes at a time when food systems are experiencing huge change. An increasingly industrialized and globalized food chain challenges the connections to food production, the environment, and fellow human beings. Urban dwellers with food accessed from a homogenized, anonymous system can forget that foods have seasons, that producing food takes great effort and knowledge, and that aspects of the landscape in which a food is produced can *actually* be tasted in the food itself. Since travel is generally promoted as a contrast to daily routine, and images of tourist destinations woo visitors by being distinctive, unusual, and exotic, traditional foodways that seem to maintain essential connections between food, family, community and landscape are very appealing. Communities where local food systems still appear to be relatively intact are attractive to tourists because they are both exotic in comparison to urban realities, and considered authentic, something tourists desire as part of their experience. The use of food and heritage in destination branding is powerful in promoting an "authentic" experience. As National Geographic travel advertises, the best holiday is one where the visitor gains an insider's perspective by experiencing things like food that reflect the local character.

Another buzz word in the travel industry is "transformation." Travel slogans promise that "everything is better on vacation," where you can be reinvigorated by stepping out of your regular routine and experiencing places that stimulate, awe, and excite the senses. A vacation can shine a spotlight on elements of one's life that are lackluster; a 2013 survey conducted by Monster.com concluded that seventy percent of people are more likely to look for another job after returning from vacation. While the personal transformation of visitors is well recognized, what is less often discussed beyond academic circles is the considerable power that tourism wields to transform what it is consuming. The phenomenon of tourists constructing stereotypical representations of destinations and then expecting them when they visit is called the "Tourist Gaze." Unlike the educational focus of the Grand Tour, critical tourism studies reveal that many of today's leisure travelers generally want to be amused and entertained, experience the beautiful, have a sense of fellowship with people, satisfy curiosity, and participate in history. This wish list shapes the anticipation of tourists and their expectations about their experience. It also sets in motion a dynamic between visitor and host that has the potential to compromise one to please the other. Add the vulnerabilities of a struggling economy, and this dynamic is amplified.

Tourism has embraced the idea of commodifying elements of cultural landscapes to make them appealing to visitors. Since tourists tend to seek "authentic" experiences in keeping with their pre-conceived ideas, when it comes to commodifying cultural heritage this is often defined as something that appears unchanged, a throwback to "yesteryear." Trevalling to find some agreeable form of the past dates back to the Grand Tour; Alphonse de Lamartine, a French writer, described Italy as a *"land of the past… where everything sleeps"*. This is problematic because culture is always changing. Italian cuisine is a case in point, reflecting a rich history of new ingredients introduced by outside influences. Tomato sauce seems to be quintessentially Italian, and it is, despite the fact that tomatoes are indigenous to Mexico and were introduced to southern Italy by the Spanish in the 1500s. Tourists often define an authentic experience as one that has been untouched by time, and catering to these stereotypes can lead to defining tradition as something stagnant and stuck in the past. This threatens to destroy these cultural traditions by transforming them into performances. I have personally encountered this viewpoint while helping to facilitate food workshops with Messors. A participant took pictures of an elderly woman expertly leading a pasta-making workshop in the kitchen of the old farmhouse where we were staying, and posted them to Facebook. There were many enthusiastic comments about getting to experience "real" Italian life, but one follower commented, disappointedly, about the microwave visible in the background, a modern appliance that apparently compromised the narrative of stepping into the Past. The next time I helped facilitate the same workshop in the same kitchen, there was much discussion about whether to move the microwave out of view of tourists and their cameras, a clear expression of the perceived need to curate an experience for tourists to meet their expectations.

Building the "Myth of Tuscany"

Tuscany offers an interesting example of the transformative power of tourism, the commodification of the rural (particularly culinary tourism), and the resulting vulnerabilities. Historically the region was quite poor, and like regions in southern Italy, experienced acceleration in the decay of small scale farming in the 1950s as farmers abandoned food production to search for work in larger cities. But Italians value highly the traditions and foods of small food producers (and the integrated concept of culture and landscape), and by 1985 a national law defined *agriturismo*, whereby farmers could supplement their farming income by adding accommodation and other farm- and food-related opportunities for tourists. The legislation recognized agritourism as an agricultural activity, and farms across Italy have been growing tourism as a new crop in increasing numbers ever since. Rural homes and buildings abandoned in the course of the rural exodus since World War II started to be reoccupied, farmhouse Bed and Breakfasts popped up, and wineries built tasting rooms. The branding was focused on the creation and revival of cultural identity based on local food products, food heritage, and rural lifestyles, all incredibly important things to preserve and promote for locals as well as tourists.

Over the past thirty years Tuscany has become a leader in agritourism and this has been a significant contributor to the region's iconic tourism identity. ISTAT data from 2015 indicate that twenty percent of farms in Tuscany are engaged in agritourism, double the number reported in 2009 and well above the national average. The region is *the* hot travel destination in Italy, especially for food lovers. Respected travel guides like Fodor's describe this destination as Italy Heaven, where you can expect *"rich wines and historic towns, some of the world's greatest works of art, rolling hills covered with olive groves and vineyards, scatterings of villas and farmhouses..."* Other media such as books and movies have also helped craft the "Myth of Tuscany" for American visitors. Frances Mayes's book *Under the Tuscan Sun* (turned into a movie) fueled the romance of Tuscany, and the idea of personal transformation in travel--and Tuscany in particular--continues to inspire. Canadian designer icon Debbie Travis recently bought and restored a 13th century farmhouse as a reality TV show that now welcomes guests for exclusive women's retreats.

Tourism has brought many economic benefits to the region. It has clearly created opportunities for younger family members who can speak and write in English, a common language of tourism. The renovations of farm buildings to accommodate agritourism enterprises have employed many small business and local craftspeople, which boosts the economy beyond the boundaries of the farm. However, the power of the Tourist Gaze has slowly shifted the focus away from primarily benefiting local food producers to attending to the trends set by the global tourism industry and catering to the demands of consumers. The rules for agritourism were originally to focus on the farm, whereby tourism was an add on, meant to create another revenue stream to support the rural economy and keep youth from migrating to the city to seek employment. But slowly there has been a separation of agritourism from agricultural activities, supported by more recent laws meant to harmonize Italian legislation with that of the EU Rural Development Objectives and Programs. Agritourism now comes in different forms that range from staying at a former farm that has been transformed to wholly serve the tourist, through to the most participatory where tourists stay at a working farm and experience authentic farm activities. In addition to the main *agriturismo* enterprises, there are now cooking classes, food tours featuring markets and producers, and other leisure activities such as horseback riding, hiking, morning yoga and massages, all designed to help attract tourists and promote the key food components of the Tuscan identity. Many argue that the EU Rural Development Program (2007-2013) has not done much to support small enterprises, and national laws are stimulating commercial agritourism that conforms to offering comforts and modern services. When agritourism is considered, first and foremost, as an instrument for economic growth and a solution to the employment and revenue problems of rural zones, a holistic perspective of the foodway has been sacrificed and the vulnerabilities of commodification are obscured. When "rural" becomes merchandise, agritourism is shaped by market demands. This can be positive; a benefit has been that farms that had become more homogenized as part of their industrialization are now planting a wider variety of crops to meet the needs of revitalized "typical products," a win not only for heirloom food varieties but also local biodiversity. However, in other respects commodification can compromise the cultural aims of locals hoping to promote and maintain rural lifestyles and the identity value of being a food producer. With a focus on romantic simplicity and tradition, local culture can easily become theatre. You want romantic, ancient, pure, untouched, and friendly (almost family-like) culture? Welcome to Tuscany, where the food is pure, good and plentiful, meals stretch out for hours, and even a tourist can get a heady sense of community and "authentic" traditions. Tuscany has become the exotic "Other," perceived as the promised land of untarnished ancient traditions, a much needed antidote to counter the stressful elements of a fast paced, modern life.

Rural Tuscany, reinvented for the 21st century, seems to be squarely within the Tourist Gaze; how else can you explain the contradictions of associating words like "countryside, farmer, rural" with "nobility, comfort, refinement" on Italy's *Agriturismo* promotion website? Tourists may want to "get away from it all" and enjoy a rustic experience, but they still expect much of their urban lifestyle in these contexts. Modern tourists, especially the influx of affluent North American and British travelers paying top dollar, expect private bathrooms, Wi-Fi, air conditioning, and other amenities, and hopeful entrepreneurs have scrambled to accommodate. Gardens are transformed to make room for the "relaxation services" of swimming pools and spas (ISTAT statistics from 2009 indicate that 37% of agritourism farms in Italy had pools). This highlights the vulnerability of rural populations that hope to promote both economic and cultural success via tourism, yet are bound to the power relationship whereby the tourist dictates what they want to consume.

Economic power plays an important role here, and the resulting representations, carefully curated to meet the wants and needs of the tourist customer, can erase inconvenient truths. In a concerted rebranding effort, *la cucina povera* (loosely translated as "poverty food" but more fairly the food of rural peasants) has become the darling of the tourism industry. Nowhere has this been capitalized on more than in Italy, where the Tourist Gaze can get a bit misty-eyed as it conjures a romantic image of utopian rural life and food cultures. Despite the broad geography and ethnic diversity of the Mediterranean (at least sixteen countries border the Mediterranean Sea, representing tremendous cultural, ethnic, religious, and economic variation), a singular diet has emerged that is often juxtaposed with the Western (North American) diet. The Mediterranean diet (of which *la cucina povera* is Italy's generalized variant), interpreted by a North American audience, has earned prime real estate on bookstore shelves. A disenchantment with the industrial food system has led many to cast their gaze rather longingly to the Mediterranean, where one sees populations drinking wine daily, consuming large quantities of olive oil, cheese, bread and generally an abundance of whole foods (especially vegetables), and living long, relatively healthy lives. Industrialized urbanites on vacation often feel nostalgia for country food, and the clichés and stereotypes of food and lifestyle weave a powerful myth of a rural paradise. As culinary tourists in Tuscany have related to anthropologist Janet Chrzan: *"If only I could live like this at home--with the Mediterranean diet and lifestyle--I'd be so healthy and happy."*

Historically, *la cucina povera* was simple, local, and seasonal. In Tuscany cheeses and milk were seasonal and chickens and eggs were available from spring to the end of autumn. Beef was an absolute luxury and reserved for the elite, and meat overall was rare for peasants, who had access to organ meats and tripe, and the occasional meals of pork (fresh in the autumn, salted or preserved at other times). Salted cod was a staple in Tuscany because it was a cheap form of protein. In his book *Delizia!*, John Dicke points out that the poverty of the peasant diet is echoed in Italian proverbs: "*when the peasant eats a chicken, either the peasant is ill, or the chicken is.*" It's easy to forget that peasants of the not-so-distant past lived in the shadow of hunger and consumed fresh, local, and seasonal food not because of moral elitism but because they ate what was available. According to Lucy Long, foods "*frequently represent a highly selective past, and sometimes an invented one.*" Tourists to rural Italy experience incredible abundance and beautiful food, including lots of fresh meat (pork, horse, beef), which is more of the tourist Mediterranean diet, constructed to cater to the tourists' expectations and cultural ideologies (and mirroring the affluent Western diet and, increasingly, the modern Italian diet).

The need for authenticity can be at odds with other tourist demands. Modern studies have concluded that many travelers like to find the familiar cuisine of home and will not travel to places that do not offer these options. There is considerable pressure to manipulate tourist cuisine to meet demands and expectations, since accommodating the wants and needs of tourists makes very good economic sense. This is on display in complimentary hotel breakfasts in southern Italy: bacon and scrambled eggs are on the menu for North American and British tourists, and you will find butter on the table in a world dominated by olive oil.

So for tourists, all is pleasing, beautiful, and stress-free. Every effort is made to make it so for tourists, to build the brand, and to get good reviews on Trip Advisor; it is easy to see how fantasies are created. The hosts need to be profitable and therefore construct identities that meet the expectations of tourists, but that may not be meaningful or useful to locals. Experiences are carefully constructed to promote the brand, and in this way culture can become a performance that is rolled out for tourists to consume but is no longer meaningful to the locals for anything other than economic profit. Tourism is not reality in this sense; it is not reality for the tourists, who do not have their regular constraints, but also not the reality of Tuscans so much as something shaped by tourist expectations. What is real though are the consequences. When revenue generation is the top priority, tourism can not only damage the "soul of the place," but it can ignore some of the real costs, which generally are paid for by locals. Tourism places new demands on water and energy use, and generates waste. Sustainable tourism tries to reduce this, but it can be hard when meeting the expectations of tourists is prioritized. For example, is it acceptable to serve leftovers to paying guests? The ethic of wasting nothing is an authentic one in rural Italy, out of necessity, but can conflict with the etiquette of how to look after important visitors.

Tourism development in Italy's south: avoiding the myth of Mezzogiorno

Agritourism has been influential in putting Tuscany on the tourist map, and Italy's south (known as the Mezzogiorno) is actively embracing this form of tourism in the hopes of improving its depressed economy. Tuscany's experiences with agritourism offer a useful model for thinking about the introduction of heritage tourism (and specifically food-related tourism) to other regions of Italy seeking to address the same rural issues of modernity. Evaluated through an economist's lens, tourism is successful at meeting its measured goals (employment, increased standard of living, and the ability to accumulate material wealth). Despite significant shifts towards industrialism since World War II, southern Italy has remained predominantly agricultural and continues to lag behind the north economically. Unemployment rates in the south are two and a half times as high as in the north (the youth unemployment rate in Basilicata is a staggering 38%.) This fuels out-migration as youth move to urban centres looking for work, and the decay of critical social and subsistence structures that result from this. Economic development is critical, and tourism offers the potential for cultural maintenance and revitalization, which is very attractive. But at what cost? It is clear that tourism can increase the awareness of food heritage for both visitors and locals, encouraging community pride and strengthening local identity, even if these food products are no longer commonly consumed by locals. It is important to recognize, though, that this objective can be at odds with the representations demanded by the Tourist Gaze. What are the consequences for the locals whose cultural practices and built and natural environments are the essential ingredients of these representations? How can the negative elements be addressed, so that locals benefit from the economic infusion that comes from tourism without selling themselves out? The damage is often hard to see until it is well under way, which makes it even more important to learn from the time depth of Tuscany's embrace of tourism.

Messors: a model for small scale, local tourism

As the south is "discovered" by a new type of tourist, businesses are hoping to both catch the wave and direct it to avoid it becoming a destructive tsunami. Messors is a small company based in Altamura that offers a combination of hands-on art restoration and culinary tourism workshops to showcase and explore various elements of the region's cultural heritage.

Unlike a bus tour, where visitors are shown a place rather passively, seeing disconnected parts without really understanding the relationships between them, Messors seeks to create opportunities for a visitor to appreciate firsthand the profound connections between humans, cultural traditions, and the landscape that can still be tasted in the food. For a culinary workshop, this means meeting the cheese maker, the baker, the butcher, the farmer, and the shepherd, and spending some time in their worlds to see the art, science, and magic that goes into their craft. I have experienced Messors first hand, from various perspectives; in 2014 I participated in a food workshop that I then helped facilitate in 2015 and 2016. In addition to contributing my knowledge and perspective as a food anthropologist, this created an opportunity for me to study the realities of this emerging economy in southern Italy and to evaluate both the promise and critiques of food tourism for myself.

It is clear from the outset that Messors' founder, Tonio Creanza, has a different approach to tourism than many others. For starters, he is uncomfortable calling visitors with Messors "tourists," preferring instead the term "participants," in recognition of the co-production of the experience. Tonio is a local providing an intimate tour of *his* landscape, which is very different from other tour companies that may not have local guides and facilitators. His role is similar to the *Cicerone* of the Grand Tour, a knowledgeable tutors who helped guide the intellectual self-improvement of the experience. His expertise and ability to connect with local food producers that he has known his entire life easily satisfies the tourist demands for authenticity. Participants are introduced to a host of food artisans who graciously invite them to try shaping the dough for famous Altamura bread, make sausages and various cheeses, and blend local ingredients together for delicious meals served outside, family-style. Tonio is an artist, and a romantic; even picnics deserve china plates and flowers at a Messors workshop, and his choice of locations for meals is imaginative and always gorgeous. Dinners are set outside as often as weather will allow, and sometimes, after a late evening meal, Tonio will pull out his guitar and play. Often he can get a local owl to sing along with him when he whistles. As you sip homemade *limoncello* the rest of the world seems to melt away into the warm night.

To be successful, Messors must comply with many of the expectations of the Tourist Gaze, which is accomplished with beautiful settings and delicious food. However, the intimate, learning-through-doing ethic gently redirects this gaze in a way that creates a more well-rounded expression of modern rural identity. This holds the promise of capturing all the benefits of culinary tourism as sustainable economic and social development while minimizing the threat of hollow performance that can creep in when culture is commodified. While the tendency of cultural tourism is to present the experience in a tourist-friendly format, unstaged authenticity should add to the overall experience. Farm-based tourism allows visitors to witness agricultural work up close, which will inevitably include barnyard smells and early morning wake ups from the sound of sheep assembling to be milked. Rather than sanitizing the experience to make it more "comfortable" for tourists, these realities should be celebrated as the reality of producers involved in making the food that will be part of a future meal. With Messors, a trip to meet and work alongside the baker starts with a 4:30 a.m. wake up call. This hardly sounds like the schedule of someone on vacation, because it isn't; it's the rhythm of the bread and the oven and the baker, who began making the dough at 2:00 a.m. to have it come out of the cavernous wood fired oven in time for the day's customers. In this way the baker is not performing, but instead is going about his daily routine and tourists are invited to fit into this reality instead of the other way around. Interestingly, creating opportunities that potentially "inconvenience" an individual on vacation promotes the authenticity that tourists want. Participants in Messors workshops are given what amounts to a "backstage pass" when they are encouraged to help in the kitchen or learn how bread is made rather than just eating the finished products. This is immensely satisfying to the visitor and maintains the integrity of food producers and builds a connection between outsiders and locals.

A core philosophy for Messors is the desire to promote and preserve the cultural knowledge that is embedded in the complex relationships between people, their food, and their landscape. Not only do these workshops provide opportunities for tourists to experience and learn about food heritage, but the interest from outsiders helps to dignify these traditions, with the hope that youth will take an interest in learning and perpetuating these cultural practices. Shepherding offers a good example of this. The livelihoods of farmers and shepherds have been woven together across the limestone Murgia Plateau of the southern peninsula for thousands of years. Historically their wool and dairy products were important components of local economies, but a combination of factors have eroded the viability of shepherding as a livelihood. A particular challenge is the sweeping set of EU regulations meant to address food safety that are blunt instruments and not realistic (or all that necessary) for small producers, leaving them with limited options. Selling the raw milk can mean that shepherds work hard for next to nothing, or quietly (and illegally) sell these cheeses from their farms as part of the local, informal economy. With such hard work and such tenuous compensation, it's hard to find many Italian youth who dream of shepherding as a career choice. A growing number of shepherds in Italy are immigrants from Eastern Europe or India; as wage labourers they are vulnerable to exploitation while keeping the price of milk low.

Tourism may be an important element in rediscovering the economic value of the knowledge, products, and landscapes of shepherds. Maintaining the shepherding landscapes by rebranding shepherd's tracks (*tratturi*) as hiking trails (as discussed in chapter 9) may be successful for both shepherds needing grazing land for their animals and visitors looking for authentic experiences. Beyond the landscapes though, a concerted effort is also needed to maintain the shepherds themselves, and the knowledge embedded in a tradition now largely sustained by elder shepherds and immigrants. The Fornello Project, affiliated with Messors, aims to apply the philosophy of participatory agritourism to generate benefits for both local shepherds of the Murgia Plateau and visiting tourists. This holistic endeavor envisions heritage as something living and contemporary rather than something frozen in time, and the long term goal is to restore the built heritage of the Fornello site located just outside of Altamura, reinstate shepherding activities in the area, and in so doing help re-establish its relevance in a modern frame.

The location for the project, the Fornello site (which means "little oven"), is a place that has been occupied by humans since the 3rd century BC. It is located less than ten kilometers from Altamura, in a landscape pockmarked by caves, their entrances obscured by vegetation. Inside, the interconnected caves tell a story of centuries of land use. This is a great example of an ancient rupestral settlement that has been dug into the tufa limestone on the side of a low, rocky hill overlooking a small pocket of fertile land in the valley bottom. Shepherds have used these caves for centuries to shelter their animals, and several caves were repurposed by Byzantine monks who were fleeing persecution in the Baltics. One cave was a church, with a rectangular nave and a niche for an altar at one end. Several skylights would have brought shafts of daylight into this underground space, lighting up the painted frescos on the cave walls. At least three layers of frescos can be seen, which are peeling away from the walls because of the salts that leach through the porous limestone. They date from AD 1100, 1200, and 1350, and suggest that this was once a form of monastery for the foreign but short-lived religious community that established itself in Puglia centuries ago. The most visible face is that of Magdalene, whose big staring eyes and subtle smile gaze down from a carved pillar in the centre of the cave. But upon closer inspection one sees remnants of other scenes, including one where a Serbian king, his ethnicity identified by his distinctive crown, gives Jesus a model replica of a round church while the baby rests in the arms of the Virgin Mary.

Above the caves is a stone shepherd's house, once used as a place to live and make cheese but abandoned for at least 150 years. An abandoned *masseria* crumbles at the crest of the hill overlooking the fertile lands to the northwest and Altamura beyond. A narrow road, considered a *tratturo*, runs between the *masseria* and the dairy building, the stone walls of the road tumbling down amongst prickly pear cacti and merging with the rocky landscape. Tonio and his partners bought the land in 2012 with the hope of restoring the built heritage of the site through re-establishing its relevance. It is an ambitious and long term plan, and sees heritage as something living and contemporary rather than something frozen in time. Unlike the modern rebirth of Matera, where heritage tourism threatens to commemorate a vanished culture and people, the Fornello project seeks to maintain continuity in the use and meaning of the site, redefined for the 21st century. This starts by re-establishing cheese making at Fornello in small, hands-on workshops. Milk is purchased from local shepherds at twice the going rate, and the craft of cheese making is maintained in the stone shepherd's dairy that has been swept out, graced with a few pieces of furniture, and re-inhabited with new purpose. The wheels of pecorino cheese are aged in one of the many caves located in the soft tufa limestone below the building, restoring some of the historic functionality of the area. Because EU regulations do not allow this cheese to be sold, it is gifted to supporters of the project, whose donations finance the perpetuation of the project and restoration of the many heritage elements of the site. The objective is to meet the needs of both visitors and shepherds. Visitors want an authentic, exclusive experience, where they can connect with food producers and learn about local food traditions. The shepherds need the ability to sell their milk for a higher price, and benefit from being re-inscribed on the landscape. The hope is to demonstrate interest that can lead to a local revival in shepherding traditions.

Interacting with locals creates a dialogue that promotes the value of cultural knowledge in a modern, rapidly changing world. This explicit recognition by outsiders of the economic and social value of integrated elements of culture can be profoundly meaningful. According to one local in Altamura, whose family has been shepherding for generations, the genuine interest of visitors in shepherding and other foodways dignifies these traditions. The pride that is demonstrated, which shines when others appreciate and are interested, is critical to the ongoing success of these cultural traditions. If there is perceived value in these professions and the knowledge that goes with them, young people are more likely to pursue them rather than casting them off as expressions of "backward" rural life incompatible with a modern reality. It shouldn't be an either-or proposition.

For Messors-style tourism to work there must be a re-framing of the tourist as guest rather than customer. As a guest they are not consumers, or passive viewers, but a traveler invited to observe, listen, smell, and taste a place on the terms of the local host. This form of dynamic tourism acknowledges participation and co-production in an experience that is meaningful for everyone. Tonio uses the metaphor of transhumance to describe his vision for tourism. With transhumance shepherds would go to different places to nourish their animals, but would leave their stories and elements of language. Their animals left manure that was fertilizer for the next crop. In this case the traveler visits a place as a source of nourishment but leaves something that enriches both people and places. This can be monetary, but it can also be something less tangible, a knowledge exchange that highlights a common, shared humanity and ignites pride or curiosity.

This becomes a very different type of experience for everyone involved. For less flexible travelers, this is challenging, particularly when things do not conform to expectations and timetables. There can be a sense of disappointment in not getting what was expected from a trip itinerary if the baker is ahead of schedule and has shaped most of the loaves by the time visitors arrive, or the shepherd anticipated to join the group for lunch comes late, or can't stop because the animals are on the move. This is hard for the tour operator, who is balancing the expectations of paying guests while honouring the natural rhythms of food producers. It can feel less organized than many travelers expect, leading to frustration. For the more adventurous, this is intoxicating: one clearly feels and understands Tonio's desire to protect his culture, promote it, share it, and make this model of tourism work for himself as a businessperson but also his broader community. A recurring comment from Messors participants was that they had enjoyed an experience like no other, so much more than a vacation, and very clearly transformative. I heard one participant say, *"Tonio, I don't have much, but anything I have is yours."*

Messors offers one example of what small scale, locally-focused tourism can look like, and how it can be beneficial both to visitors and local food producers. But being sustainable *must* also include being economically successful, and even Messors feels the pressure to be profitable and attract more participants. It's easy to start making decisions based on how participants will perceive things, or how a dinner location will photograph for Facebook and Instagram promotion. Creating fantastic, memorable experiences is a huge amount of work, and sometimes pulling off the magic can be at the expense of health and interpersonal relationships. As a small business, Messors feels key vulnerabilities of the tourism industry. World events like the turbulent global economy since 2008, sharp changes in the value of currencies, safety concerns associated with terrorist activity in Europe, and the unrest tied to the ongoing refugee crisis can make tourists re-evaluate their travel plans. These factors, like the weather for a farmer, are beyond a tourism operator's control, but have significant consequences that ripple through communities that have come to depend on this contribution to their economy.

Tourism's millennial future

Despite the shortcomings of commodification, three things stand out in this expression of sustainable culinary tourism: awareness, appreciation, and participation. Taken together, they impart a special tourist experience that is both enjoyable and valuable to everyone involved. It is impossible to make your own food without becoming aware of the human connections that link the land to the food and the people. In the context of the industrial food system, it is unusual to be able to connect so closely with food producers. Reconnecting consumers and producers creates an appreciation for the effort and knowledge that is required to make food that is good, clean, and fair, the watchwords of the Slow Food Movement. While Slow Food is a complex organization with cultural and political motivations, its mantra of "good, clean and fair" is useful for summarizing the dawning awareness that can happen as tourists engage with their food in new ways. The food that Messors shares with participants is "good" because it is made from scratch with fresh ingredients, generally purchased directly from producers who infuse their stories into their products. It is "clean" because of its environmental footprint; it is local, seasonal, and in many cases promotes the maintenance of a landscape, be it in terms of soil erosion (like lemon gardens) or biodiversity (shepherding), that has broad benefits. Finally, it is "fair" because in appreciating the amount of effort required to produce the food, a consumer is more likely to pay the real price of a product, providing more of a living wage for producers.

The potential benefits of tourism are varied and significant. In fact, the United Nations proclaimed 2017 as the International Year of Sustainable Tourism for Development *"in recognition of the tremendous potential of the tourism industry, which accounts for some 10% of the world's economic activity, to contribute to the fight against poverty and foster mutual understanding and intercultural dialogue."* The trick is to make sure that holidays do not become an experience run by tourists, directed by tourists, and primarily in the interests of tourists, since such enterprises generally do not lead to widespread benefits for locals. Many in the south are keenly aware of this difficult balance. A colleague in Altamura, whose credentials are in tourism, told me that he no longer visits Florence or Venice because these cities are shells of their former selves, designed to fit and meet the expectations of tourists. He passionately argued that despite having a vested interest in tourism being successful in Puglia, he would rather it not attract visitors than destroy the town that he holds so dear.

It is no surprise that part of the Myth of Tuscany that is so compelling for tourists is the idea of being more connected to community and food production, a stark contrast to most North American realities. The fast-paced lifestyle that is selected for and then required to support a fiercely independent, consumer culture can feel impersonal and out of touch with life's more basic elements: food, family, community, and landscape. Increasingly, North Americans do not grow their own food, or know people who do, and families are scattered across a broad geography to better access personal opportunities like school and work. Investing in personal success is valued over the shared benefits that come from more communal investments. This sense of Paradise Lost fuels nostalgia in travelers and a desire to experience a utopian, "simple life" in rural travel destinations, one seemingly untarnished by the harsh trade-offs of modernity.

Brush away the rural myth though, and you will see the same things happening in southern Italy that North Americans are responding to: this landscape is not isolated in a bubble. When communities are fractured by family members moving away to cities or even other countries looking for work, it is difficult to find people with the moral obligation to participate in food production work in a reciprocal way. Workers must be hired to harvest the olives and the grapes that are made into olive oil and wine, which can make maintaining small family groves and vineyards prohibitively expensive. This then accelerates the trend of small farmers selling out, and larger corporate producers moving in, or farms being abandoned altogether. A tourist in rural Italy can contribute to sustainable economic development, but can also appreciate the modern challenges of maintaining the cultural traditions that are considered so novel and appealing to the outsider. What a great opportunity to look at these processes and critically evaluate our own realities at home, to not only dignify and support the perpetuation of these key cultural elements in Italy, but to think about how to do the same after the vacation comes to an end. This awareness, this sense of connection, means that visitors may go home and shop at farmers' markets, and have a better understanding of why small farmers charge more for their high quality products, and so invigorate their own local foodways. The knock-on effect is significant.

Thinking critically about agricultural and heritage-based tourism is timely; the Italy's south is experiencing a surge in tourist interest. Hoping to cash in on the Tourist Rush, entrepreneurs are transforming *masserie*--large stone farmhouses--into boutique hotels, and the list of "guest services" that are now expected can be challenging to offer. In a landscape where water has always been scarce, the burden of tourists expecting fresh towels and bed linens every day will be borne by locals. Providing air conditioning and central heating for year round comfort will be incredibly expensive given the price of electricity. Sanitizing the rural landscape to conform to the sleek modern definition of "luxury" may actually compromise its ability to offer an "authentic," exclusive experience. Tourists may want the farm atmosphere but not the farm reality. Reshuffling priorities to suit the tourist consumer can lead to a carefully curated version of a pastoral landscape, yet remove the sounds and smells of animals to appease guests, and these landscapes cease to be working farms. This style of luxury accommodation, and the associated food and wine-based activities offered to guests, can end up looking the same, a standardized, homogenized set of products based on the supposed needs and expectations of the paying customer. The effect is that farms shift to growing tourist experiences, and nothing else.

Historical underdevelopment of the region creates the potential for vulnerability and exploitation based on power dynamics and the perceived need to give tourists what they are looking for. Successful sustainable tourism, both economically and culturally, will meet the expectations of tourists while maintaining meaningful local identities and cultural practices, which can be a tall order. If tourists expect a romantic throwback to the past, when things were "pure, simple, and healthy," one of two things will happen: first, they will be disappointed to see microwaves and other expressions of modernity, or second, tourism enterprises will carefully script the tourist experience to hide these "inauthentic" components from the Tourist Gaze. Neither of these are very positive outcomes, particularly if the dictates of outsiders stagnate tradition into dusty relics from an imagined past. What is encouraging though is that success depends on knowing your audience, and the audience is changing. A number of recent studies suggest that there is a growing demand for a new type of tourism, one that is environmentally, culturally, and economically sustainable. The demand is coming from Millennials, a generation that has been unfairly stereotyped as self-centred, lazy, and looking for a good party. In reality, Millennials are quite interested in sustainability, community, creativity and entrepreneurship, more so than their parents' generation. This makes them a special kind of tourist, and since they are expected to account for half of all global travel spending by 2020, the industry ignores them at their peril. Millennials appear to be giving big mainstream hotels and restaurants a miss, looking instead for the hidden gems that make you feel like you've stumbled upon a local's favourite, providing an insider's experience. They want local experiences rather than luxury ones, and when it comes to food, they celebrate the concept of farm to table and craft beer, and support local artisans. In 2014, Forbes magazine commented that Millennials not only want to know how and where their food is produced, they want to enjoy food as a shared experience. Since statistics show that culinary tourists in general spend more for their experience, the culinary tourism industry is looking like a rosy economic opportunity.

Equally encouraging is the conclusion that education-based travel is well suited to culinary tourism, as the typical food tourist is often the well-educated professional with the disposable income to not only enjoy travel but the interest in a "professional vacation," where one learns something that helps with personal development. This should create a unique opportunity for successful economic and cultural development that moves beyond the fantasy to give tourists an authentic experience in a modern context. In multiple, small ways Messors and other culinary tourism enterprises can introduce travelers to real, meaningful local identities by highlighting the "fantasies" and omissions that are common in the Tourist Gaze, and emphasizing how these identities and traditions are produced by everyone, including tourists. It has been noted in other contexts that programs meant to support heritage often benefit only those consuming it (like the tourists), or those who profit directly from tourism instead of the indigenous groups that supply the "backbone of continuity" to the ancient foodways. Tourism can be cast as a form of neocolonialism, a hegemonic act shaped by capitalist agendas, but equally possible is to think of tourism as an opportunity for empowerment, where the curiosity that fuels tourists creates an opening for producers to dignify their foodways by sharing them with a receptive and respectful audience. It is clear that tourism commodifies foodways, which comes with great responsibilities and potential vulnerabilities. If done carefully, tourism can leverage the resources of the affluent traveler and support local development while offering experiences that are positive for everyone.

4. Matera

Matera is a spectacular town of 60,000 residents in Basilicata in southern Italy. The city stretches along the southern slopes of a deep ravine with a labyrinth of small caves carved out of a layer of soft limestone. From the far side of the ravine, you can truly appreciate Matera in its entirety. The most complex and oldest part of the town is centred around the cathedral, located at the highest point. Habitation in the surrounding area stretches back to the Paleolithic (including Altamura Man found nearby that may date to 130,000 years ago). Matera is one of many rupestral (*rupes* meaning rock) settlements in the region that take advantage of the local geology, but here the mass of soft limestone has provided the opportunity for a concentration of settlement, which is what makes Matera unique. Humans have inhabited caves here for at least the last 9,000 years, making it one of the oldest continuously occupied cities in the world, second only to Aleppo in Syria. Initial settlement was in the natural caves in the ravine walls. These were gradually extended until thousands of grottos honeycombed the area beneath the town. The dialogue between positive (building) and negative (excavating) architecture gives Matera its complexity and influences life in the town. Caves were carefully enlarged by quarrying the soft tufa limestone in blocks that were then used for construction of above ground structures.

Today, the old part of Matera along the ravine, the series of caves called *sassi* ("stony wards"), is organized into two neighbourhoods: Caveoso and Barisano. Newer parts of the ancient city lie behind them and stretch away

A view across the rooftops of the dense sasso Barisano. The cross from the Chiesa di San Pietro Caveoso is visible to the left.

from the ravine across a fairly flat plain. Matera epitomizes the story of the entire south, and offers an excellent reflection of the changing fortunes of inhabitants that have always been bound by their relationship to the landscape.

From the earliest true villages that sprouted in the Neolithic, inhabitants adapted to a fairly challenging environment. The limestone geology of the Murgia Plateau and the arid climate were forces that shaped the relationship between humans and their landscape. The higher rises of rocky terrain are best used for sheep, and the shallow valleys with some arable soil are suitable for agriculture, so an integrated agro-pastoral system developed to take advantage of both. The most important infrastructure in these drylands that lack surface water was based on collecting and distributing water. Above the *sassi*, water running off the higher areas and over the clay flats was trapped and distributed to a system of tanks and cisterns dug into the limestone that held and distributed drinking water to the town. Special caves collected winter snow that could preserve food in the winter, and melted into water to be collected and used in the dry season. The water was collected at the edge of the steep sides of the ravine and then directed to the *sassi*, which was facilitated by the vertical nature of the neighbourhoods. Rainwater was captured in small bedrock tanks that could be used by passing herds of animals, or be diverted along terraces to slow the movement of the water and encourage the creation of fertile soil.

Evidence of the engineering genius of the integrated rain water and ground water collection system can still be seen at the *Palombaro Lungo*, an impressive piece of "water architecture" that is located beneath the piazza Vittorio Veneto. This massive hydraulic reservoir was one of three large *palombari* (meaning a system designed to access both rain water like a cistern as well as ground water) that stored water for the dry periods of the year. The caverns were excavated by hand beginning in the 1500s and were enlarged as the population increased, ultimately measuring 50 meters long with vaulted ceilings 16 meters high. The *palombaro* could hold up to 5 million litres of water, which would filter down through the city's gigantic hydraulic system that can be visualized like the roots of an upturned tree, with small tanks connected to larger ones; each cave house had its own small cistern and/or one shared by the courtyard.

Concerns over the weight of this amount of water in an area honeycombed with many levels of cave dwellings below led to the closure and draining of the *palombaro* in the 1920s, when the Pugliese aqueduct was built that brought water from the Sele River and the city was no longer so closely tied to the immediate environment for its water needs. This technological genius was forgotten until the 1990's, when the *palombaro* was rediscovered during construction work in the piazza. Visiting this impressive component of Matera's water management system today is like moving through an underground cathedral; the cross arch construction rises up to support the *piazza* above, and a brown line on the walls reflects the high water mark, showing a maximum depth of 14 meters.

Matera's story is one of Paradise Lost, and then found. By World War II the area was amongst the poorest in Italy. In the 1940s half of the population of approximately 20,000 that lived in the *sassi* did not have running water or sanitation. Health issues like malaria, cholera, typhoid, and malnutrition were rampant in the overcrowded *sassi* slums. The area was extremely poor. People here were portrayed by Carlo Levi (a political prisoner, writer and artist exiled to Basilicata in the 1930s) as the wretched and forgotten. As someone who did not support Mussolini's regime, he was particularly struck by the hypocrisy of the Fascist Party's "civilizing missions" in North Africa when Italians like the residents of Matera's *sassi* (and of other small towns in the region like Aliano where he lived during his exile) were so shockingly poor. This inconsistency really struck a chord and influenced his writing. In Levi's famous book, *Christ Stopped in Eboli*, which served to highlight the plight of the poor on the southern peninsula, he described the dire conditions of the town:

> *"In these dark holes, I saw a few pieces of miserable furniture, beds and some ragged clothes hanging up to dry. On the floor lay dogs, sheep, goats and pigs... Children appeared from everywhere, in the dust and heat, stark naked or in rags, eyelids red and swollen...and with the wizened faces of old men, yellow and worn with malaria, their bodies reduced by starvation to skeletons...I have never in all my life seen such a picture of poverty."*

Crumbling cave entrances are locked behind rusting metal doors.

With the popularity of Levi's book, the poverty of the south could no longer be ignored, and in the feverish push for modernity and reconstruction after the war (dubbed the Economic Miracle) the impoverished south was an embarrassment. Matera was branded the "national shame." The caves were condemned by an act of parliament in 1952 and the *sassi's* residents were forcibly relocated to newly constructed neighbourhoods. By the 1960s, the *sassi* had fallen into ruin, the caves abandoned and bricked up, crumbling, a place to throw garbage. The state owned the caves, and it was difficult to encourage investment and redevelopment. In 1993 Matera was designated a UNESCO World Heritage Site, representing "the most outstanding example of a troglodyte settlement in the Mediterranean," and since then life has begun to return to the *sassi* neighbourhoods. Matera has become a tech hub. Many of the first to re-inhabit the *sassi* were young entrepreneurs ready to locate their technology businesses in converted caves. Although many caves in the lowest part of the old town remain abandoned and overgrown, many caves have been restored as boutique hotels. How bewildering it must be for former residents, many of whom still refuse to talk about the *sassi* out of shame, to find their former cave homes transformed into shops and luxury hotels offering the exotic opportunity to sleep in a cave. (One such hotel has transformed the water-collecting cistern into a spa!)

A city reimagined in the 21ˢᵗ century

Matera is at the forefront of tourism in the province of Basilicata. Its unique beauty, paired with the architecture and extreme history, makes it a real draw. This will only intensify in the coming years, since Matera has been named the European Capital of Culture for 2019. According to the EU, this designation is "meant to highlight the richness and diversity of cultures in Europe, to celebrate the cultural features Europeans share, to increase European citizens' sense of belonging to a common cultural area, and to foster the contribution of culture to the development of cities." The point of the designation is to generate sustainable, long-term cultural and social development in the city; a city places a bid, and if it is successful, the designation comes with some money from the EU. However, the expectation is that the city will invest a significant amount in delivering the yearlong cultural programming and reliance on additional support from commercial deals (which is where the designation starts to sound a bit like the Olympics). Many believe that this recognition ignites the next phase in the city's transformation, a dynamic reinvention that has been in play since the 1940s. The bid for this recognition can be considered evidence of resilience and victory over a recent history defined by shame and poverty. According to organizers of the bid, "*although Matera is a city which has implemented a number of important regeneration schemes, as yet it has not exploited its enormous cultural potential to the full.*" The hope is that the designation will help attract both tourists and permanent cultural and technological talent, building long-term, socio-economic benefits. It is excellent exposure for Matera, and will certainly help attract large numbers of visitors from Europe and around the world. What will this new influx of tourists do to the narrow, winding streets of Matera? It is easy for tourists to walk along the polished limestone streets in awe and pass right by the more recent history of suffering, seeing only romantic decay.

Matera is actively engaged in destination branding with an emphasis on cultural wealth, shared cultural heritage, and vibrancy of the arts. What is interesting is that the platform of the ECoC is premised on the cooperative construction of a united European cultural identity based upon a continuity with, and inheritance of, a shared past. There is an interesting tension here in seeking unity by celebrating diversity. Since the inception of the program in 1985, culture capitals have been chosen for the themes that they embody that they can share with the continent. This requires some familiar narratives that, in some cases, have led to homogenization and the selection of more appealing stories. What story of the *sassi* will be part of the representation of Matera? The story that includes eviction and relocation at the great expense of language, family systems, and culture? Or will the story be one of progressive salvation? As Matera looks to the future, its modern identity is being built from the age-old themes that have been the foundation of this unique city for over 7,000 years: beauty, sustainability, resilience, and ingenuity. To truly appreciate these characteristics, and the phoenix rising out of the ashes, you must go back several chapters in the story.

Matera was not always an impoverished city. Many scholars describe Matera as one of the European capitals of the Neolithic Age, and during the Middle Ages it was considered a glorious city of historical and cultural importance. I think the most poetic depiction of this comes from Al-Idrisi, a Muslim geographer and cartographer in the court of the Norman king Roger II who explored the southern peninsula in the 12th century. Awed by the twinkling lanterns that lit the caves at night, he described the sight as the earthly reflection of a starry night sky, the constellations above mirrored in the human world.

For millennia the city thrived due to its self-sufficiency. Food was grown in roof gardens irrigated by the complex water management system. These gardens were fertilized with local animal fertilizer. Over time the town developed into the warren-like *sassi* of subterranean dwellings and churches and above ground architecture. Each cave or compound had its own water-collecting cistern (or sometimes two), the size of which reflected the amount of water that people knew to expect every winter. The genius of Matera is expressed in the use of scarce resources efficiently and sparingly, and truly reflects the connection between humans and their landscape. The infrastructure of caves, aboveground buildings constructed from tufa blocks, roof kitchen gardens, water management canals and reservoirs, and the network of trails that wove the neighbourhoods together was designed for sustainability and success in a challenging landscape.

What happened to Matera to make it descend into the misery and filth described so famously by Carlo Levi? It is only relatively recently that Matera sunk into woe, and this was due in great part to losing the connection to the landscape. The decline of sustainable habitation in the late 18th and early 19th centuries was fueled by rapid population increase and growing world trade. The flat area behind the *sassi*, a wetland in the rainy season and the site of key water management infrastructure for the *sassi*, had not been developed with buildings for good reason. However, as the city expanded to accommodate the growing population it built on this area, which meant that the elements

Al-Idrisi's twinkling, earthly constellations can still be seen as dusk descends on the sassi.

that were critical to the *sassi* infrastructure, the tanks and cisterns and water diversion features, became inaccessible and could not be maintained.

The *sassi* neighbourhoods had housed all the inhabitants of the town, with both peasant cave homes alongside large *palazzi*. But as the city grew, wealthy Materans moved up to the flat plain above the ravine. The ancient *sassi* were increasingly alienated from the residents in the new upper areas, and social inequality became inscribed in the geography of the city. The customary agreements that had maintained the sustainability of the *sassi* and managed space, water and hygiene faded, with predictable results. The location of the *sassi* on the edge of the steep ravine, combined with the growing wealthy neighbourhood above, meant that the *sassi* could not expand in size. As the peasant population swelled, the *sassi* became overcrowded and unhealthy, and the poor neighbourhoods became associated with disease and misery. Families shared their small dark cave homes with mules, pigs, and chickens, the only benefit of which was that the animals helped to warm the dank earthen homes. Large families shared small spaces and ate from a single large bowl, and hunger was ever present. As Levi remarked, the withered bodies of children were stark evidence of malnutrition.

Matera's poverty was also tied to other changes in the relationship between humans and their landscape, in particular the decline of shepherding and the protection of transhumance in the south. The Industrial Revolution

The terracotta gutter systems of Matera and the surrounding Murgia Plateau are designed like a marble-run. The water is directed off roofs and along channels in the streets so that it not only flows away from building foundations but into collection cisterns. Gravity helps distribute the water through Matera's vertical neighbourhoods.

and era of European colonization of huge chunks of the globe saw the development of complex economies and a new global division of labour that had far-reaching effects. For centuries shepherding products had been highly valued in the South as important sources of protein and wool for textiles. When Australia was colonized by the British, and their sheep industry could provide a cheaper product, it became a key supplier of wool to the English textile industry (and ultimately the largest supplier of wool in the world). This competition and resulting decline in wool exports undermined the economic relevance of the agro-pastoral system in southern Italy. This, in tandem with the growing demand for wheat, saw the erosion of regulations and institutions that had been designed and implemented centuries before to protect grazing rights and the critical infrastructure of the *tratturi*, corridors that facilitated the movement of flocks between pastures.

As Italy began to rebuild after World War II, Matera's extreme poverty and decay appeared out of sync with the push towards modernity. How could a country on the path to prosperity have such abject poverty in its midst? And scores of people who still lived in caves?! It also clearly highlighted the glaring differences between the North and the South, dubbed the Southern Question, which had become a heated topic of conversation in post-war Italy. It was a national disgrace, and became the focus of various development efforts to modernize and improve the standard of living of southern Italians. In 1950 the *Cassa per il Mezzogiorno*, a special ministry of the Italian government tasked with leading the investment in social and economic development of southern Italy, initiated land reform meant to transform tenant farmers into land owners. The ambitious, ten-year, $2 billion (USD) program focused on increasing agricultural yield by introducing irrigation and land transformation, increasing labour consumption, building roads to promote integration into the broader economy, and the provision of a public water supply. Taken together the goal was to improve living conditions for peasants.

The hope was that the poverty and misery could be relieved fairly quickly by land reform legislation. Land reform expropriated land from the large estates of absentee landlords and gave it to landless labourers and peasants whose holdings were too small to be self-sufficient. These measures went hand in hand with the executive order that mobilized the evacuation/eviction of the *sassi* in 1952. Famous Italian architects were commissioned to design modern rural villages near the expropriated lands to resettle *sassi* residents closer to their fields (many who lived in the *sassi* walked four to six hours a day to access their fields). Some former inhabitants of the *sassi* were moved to La Martella, located a few kilometers outside of Matera in the midst of fragments of expropriated lands. This new community received 200 families in 1953 and offered the conveniences of a "dignified," modern lifestyle. Unlike the

Abandoned caves cling to the edge of the ravine, while post-war apartment blocks overlook them in Matera's newer neighbourhoods.

near communal living of *sassi*, where families lived in their own *sassi* but shared large communal spaces outside their *sassi* entrances, each house was detached, and had 600 m² of land attached to it as a kitchen garden. Each house was also associated with a small farm, generally 6-7 hectares in size, meant to adequately support a family of five.

The *sassi* were emptied and all but forgotten for thirty years, as though centuries of history and the life and traditions that had been sustained there could be erased. While many of the land reform initiatives were not fully realized, and the goals of Italy's "Economic Miracle" only marginally met in the South, the key indicators of success were met in terms of Matera. Individuals were no longer living in cave "hovels" without running water, electricity, or basic sanitation. Health issues like typhoid and malnutrition were eradicated. Sadly, these outcomes were hard won from a social and cultural perspective. The *sassi* were not only ecologically sustainable, their design offered important social cohesion. The caves were fairly dark, so the dining and kitchen areas were located close to the door and windows, and living spilled out into the courtyards--*vicinati*--that the homes opened onto and shared with their neighbours. Generally, extended families and close, family-like neighbours shared these courtyards. These were places to work communally, gossip, and support one another. The courtyards were linked throughout the *sassi* by webs of stairways and footpaths that kept the neighbourhood connected both physically and socially. In the modern,

A courtyard, shared by many caves, with a stepped footpath that connects the upper and lower parts of the sassi.

individual housing units of La Martella, the *vicinati* that were meant to act as shared outdoor spaces were too big to replicate the *vicinati* of the *sassi*. Plus, extended family groups were not relocated together, so the long-standing social connections, mutual obligations and fellowship were lost. These social units had fostered a strong sense of inter-dependency, and sadly this old system of strength and solidarity was a casualty of the individualistic modern world. Scorn and shame for the "traditional" lifestyle left behind in the *sassi* also encouraged the adoption of standardized Italian and the local dialect, *Materano*, went silent. As modernity led to more agricultural efficiencies many farmers found themselves redundant, and it was a fairly easy switch to become apartment-living factory workers at the industrial facilities that sprang up in La Martella. The disconnect between humans and their landscape became even more pronounced.

The post-war story of Matera was echoed in other urban renewal projects. A popular concept in the US and Europe in the 1950s and 1960s saw old neighbourhoods demolished and new ones built to house displaced populations. In an ironic reversal, some of the very pre-modern qualities of the *sassi* that fueled their eviction in the 1950s are now being recast as exotic and desirable. The Italian government now sees the value of the *sassi*, and since the 1990s has offered grants to restore the same caves that were condemned and from which their occupants were forcibly dispossessed. The

UNESCO World Heritage designation has increased the perceived value of the *sassi* to both locals and tourists, and has fueled important examples of cultural rejuvenation. Reconstructing the cave dwellings has been controversial--should they be restored to their state in 1950 or something more desirable?--but these efforts have required masons to relearn stone construction methods, like building vaults. There is new interest in reviving the *Materano* dialect, a critical repository of culture and identity. And *la cucina lucana*, the local dishes of Basilicata and Matera specifically, has reappeared on restaurant menus. While many local foods like *lampascioni* (wild tasselled hyacinth bulbs) continued to be eaten after the abandonment of the *sassi*, others were not cooked for decades. Near forgotten dishes like fried, dried red peppers, mashed fava beans, fried chicory, and sweet ricotta are part of the proud revival of Matera's heritage and identity and part of its representation on the world stage.

For individuals who physically experienced the uprooting from the *sassi* and the shame of this "preindustrial" lifestyle, valuing and moving back to the caves is inconceivable. Part of moving to La Martella was leaving the past behind and keeping the eyes trained forward on a modern future. It's the grandchildren of these last *sassi* inhabitants who are starting to feel nostalgic for this past, and the identity that is bound to the *sassi*. The embrace of this forgotten past ties in quite nicely to the UNESCO designation and the economic incentives of tourism. However, casting Matera as the "Sassi City" requires some selective recollection that threatens the complex, meaningful identity of the city and its inhabitants. The focus on a peasant theme, since peasants were the primary residents of the *sassi* by the 19th century, is fairly myopic. Calling Matera "the capital of peasant civilization" omits the other segments of society that also called Matera home. And while peasants are the focal point, it is only a small slice of their life--cave living--and even then, it's a domestic life that has been cleaned up almost beyond recognition! Some cave-living realities cannot be completely erased: they smell like wet dirt after a rainstorm, and are moist and clammy, but with electricity, hot showers and Wi-Fi the modern *sassi* let visitors experience a preindustrial world without the discomforts of preindustrial conditions. There is something exotic and otherworldly about being able to stay in caves, now rehabilitated, modernized, and made romantically elegant.

Residents of Matera do not necessarily agree on how to represent Matera in the 21st century. There is a tension over how to tell Matera's story, whether (and how much) to look back, what stories to tell, and what image to promote. Can it conform to outsider perceptions and still remain relevant to locals? Some argue that the recent past is too painful to dredge up, and that its commodification to woo tourists is disrespectful. The balance is tricky--many locals are benefiting from the new tourist interest and are restoring their *sassi* homes to rent out through internet platforms like Airbnb. These young Materans are turning themselves into entrepreneurs and finding ways to make the most of their circumstances and create jobs that will keep them close to their families. Paola and Guiseppe, for example, are a brother and sister team who have slowly renovated their family's cave home in Sasso Barisano to create a revenue opportunity. They now have a room and small apartment that they have rented out since 2010 to visitors looking to live in the *sassi* for a few days. They are incredibly proud of their city and their personal restoration efforts, and welcome visitors with open hearts (and a cappuccino in the morning on the terrace overlooking the *sassi*). However, these small enterprises seem to be dwarfed by the exclusive hotel businesses nearby that are likely not owned by Materans, and then the benefit to locals is less clear. And when Materans are not living in the *sassi*, the steep, stepped paths of the old town home to bed and breakfasts and souvenir shops instead of the daily life of residents, the *sassi* appear to be a tourist's playground. Certainly there are many compromises that come with embracing tourism economics.

On a 2016 visit to Matera I got a clear sense of what Matera will feel like if it realizes its potential as a tourist mecca. It was a holiday, and the streets of the *sassi* were packed with Italian visitors, many of whom were being led on tours by guides brandishing umbrellas so that they could be followed more easily. It reminded me of clouds of locusts moving across a farmer's field and consuming everything in sight. It created a din, an energy, a crush that was slightly unpleasant. And yet, I too was there as a traveler, someone curious and interested and in awe of the city's beauty. I enjoyed exploring the abandoned

Cave for rent: an old space takes on a new life as an Airbnb apartment.

caves at the south end of the Barisano neighbourhood, listened intently as Francesco Festa led us on an earnest tour of his childhood cave home that he has turned into a museum. It was not until later in the evening, when the foreign crowds had subsided, that the true character of the city seemed to reemerge: people getting married and masses of locals of all ages strolling the streets.

Church bells drew us through the maze of winding streets to the cathedral, and inside a choir was readying to perform for a packed house. When the music and singing started, it filled up the cavernous building, and I could understand why cathedrals had such soaring ceilings to contain such an incredible sound. Early the next morning I relished walking the *sassi* streets alone, joined by diving swallows and the odd cat. I followed a path that switch backed its way down into the ravine, where I could get a different perspective of this ancient city with an undying, relentless spirit. The ravine was quiet and beautiful, and the city above me basked in bright sunlight like a spotlight. Tourism will no doubt cast another bright spotlight on this place, and Materans hope to make the most of the new interest in their city and the ECoC designation by consciously developing a strategic plan that emphasizes reuse and sustainable cultural investments rather than new construction. Matera is doing its best to demonstrate its resilience. Branded as a "National Shame" in the 1950s, an emblem of the backwards nature of the South in conflict with modernity, Matera now actively cultivates the themes that have been woven through the city's long history to rebrand as a model for sustainability in the 21st century and beyond. The keywords of Matera are inspiring to anyone: re-invent, re-evaluate, renew, rediscover.

5. Pasta

Life is a combination of magic and pasta.
-Federico Fellini

In a game of word association, "Italian food" would almost certainly conjure up images of pasta. Long strands of spaghetti, short macaroni, fresh or dried, pasta has become synonymous with Italy and a hallmark of Italian food culture. One can be forgiven for being surprised that Italians eat things other than pasta! It is also generally assumed that Italians invented pasta, so it is interesting to note that they perfected a tradition of great antiquity and have been mistakenly credited with the original innovation. While there is ultimately a connection to the noodles of Asia (archaeologists have discovered a 4,000 year old noodle in China), Italians were introduced to pasta by the Arabs during their conquests of Sicily in the 9th century AD. This cultural exchange has drastically influenced the region's cuisine. By the 12th century, Italians had learned the Arabian methods for drying pasta to preserve it for travel, a critical step in the success of the food. Near industrial scale production of dried pasta in the late 1700s, made possible by the development of the screw press, created unprecedented demand for wheat in the south, with important consequences in the land use balance between farmer and shepherd. The unification of Italy in 1861 fueled a significant exodus of tenant farmers and sharecroppers from southern Italy who chose the unknown of the Americas over the prospect of deepening poverty and economic and social unrest of their homeland. From 1880 to 1914 over four million Italians arrived in North America, bringing their food culture with them. Since pasta requires few ingredients and stores well when dried, it is no surprise that it became the cornerstone of Italian food identity both at home and abroad.

There is an incredible variety of regionally specific styles of pasta. Long or short, smooth or ridged, thick or thin, with or without curves and crevices, different shapes of pasta capture and absorb sauce differently. *Capuntini*, for example, are perfect little cups to trap sauce. All of this seems familiar, but there is a key difference in the way it is eaten that every visitor should be aware of: pasta is part of nearly every meal but is not the main course! When meals are presented in courses it is important not to overload on the pasta. Rest assured that another dish (and the meat dish if one is being served) follows.

All pasta in Puglia is made with durum wheat flour. With only two ingredients (unless it is pasta that is rolled out in which case egg is added), Pugliese pasta are often touted as part of the poverty roster. This does not make it any less delicious, and, in fact, the high protein content of durum wheat means that egg is not necessary as a binder, somewhat recasting the interpretation of *"la cucina povera."*

Basic Pugliese pasta dough

2 parts coarse durum wheat flour (semolina)
1 part fine durum wheat flour
Warm water

Capunti and *capuntini* are made with a combination of coarse and fine durum wheat. Water is mixed into a well of flour and thoroughly kneaded for 10-15 minutes until the dough is smooth and stiff. The dough is hard to work, but kneading is very important to develop the gluten structure. Patience is a key ingredient here to ensure the dough is kneaded enough so that it is elastic. Unlike pastry dough, pasta is worked on wooden boards across the grain because they provide a subtle grip that is needed for working the dough and shaping the pasta.

The dough is cut in chunks, then rolled out into thin strands on a dry wooden board with a small amount of flour. The trick is to use the palms of your hands and enough pressure to create a snake of dough that is an even thickness--harder than it sounds. The strands are then floured so that they do not stick together.

For *capuntini* the strands are cut into small pill-sized pieces, then individually rolled across the board with the end of your finger so that it curls up. For *capunti* a length of the strand (about the length of three finger widths) is rolled in the same way using your middle three fingers.

Two varieties of pasta commonly made in Puglia use coarse durum wheat flour and egg in the dough. An egg is cracked directly into the flour well and then fairly warm water was added and all ingredients are mixed together by hand and kneaded in rolls until smooth. A general rule seems to be 1 egg for every 100g of flour.

Orecchiete ("little ears") is a cupped pasta. Because it is labour intensive it is reserved for special occasions. The dough is rolled into fat strands, cut into pieces about 2cm long and "smeared" with a knife along the wooden board to create domed shells. To get the lip the cup is then turned inside out on the tip of your thumb. This variety was tricky; our novice efforts were poor imitations compared to Tonio's mother Grazia. *Orecchiete* should be dried upside down.

Tagliatelle is a hand-cut string pasta like *fettuccine*. The dough was rolled out expertly with a long dowel to get it perfectly thin while keeping it round. It was mesmerizing to watch the dowel roll across the pasta, then have the pasta roll up onto the dowel momentarily before it rolled back out onto the board. After letting the dough dry a bit so that the strips won't stick together, take a sharp knife and cut the dough into thin strips.

All of these pastas are best cooked fresh (after about an hour of drying) but can also be air dried for a few days and then frozen. *Buon apetito*!

6. Pizza: The taste of poverty in Italy's south

Any food enthusiast wants to eat pizza if they visit Napoli. It is is, after all, the birthplace of this iconic Italian food, made famous in an Italian-American context. Food anthropologists use the term *typicality* to identify foods that become important parts of urban brands. Parma is known for its ham and cheese, Roquefort-sur-Soulzon in France is known for its blue sheep's milk cheese, and Napoli is known for its pizza. The story of pizza is really the story of the South's largest urban centre.

Napoli's historic district is a great area to explore during the day, with narrow streets and vendors spilling out of small shops. However, wandering these streets at night looking for a pizzeria feels dangerous. Having a police officer suggest that we remove obvious jewelry even when walking in a group did not create a sense of comfort, and explains why many organized tours avoid Napoli. The city's relationship with tourists, and the role that key foods have played in this story of representation, is complex. Napoli has long been a tourist destination, but the same elements of the Industrial Revolution that enabled growing numbers of wealthy young men from England to participate in the Grand Tour in the late 18th century also brought increasing numbers of poor peasants to urban centres. This cast a grungy pall over Napoli that makes modern tour buses bypass the city in favour of safer, cleaner destinations. Since the Middle Ages, Italian cities provisioned themselves by drawing resources from the surrounding countryside. Napoli was the capital of the Kingdom of Napoli that covered much of the southern peninsula (with the exclusion of Sicily) and the system of *annona* (a complex and potentially corrupt system where city governments bought grain and then sold it to citizens at fixed prices) seems to have drained the kingdom to feed the capital. Napoli was flush with cultural and intellectual capital that is still visible today. Patrons of the arts and sciences like Raimondo di Sangro, seventh Prince of Sansevero, supported master artists of the 18th century who made the stunningly beautiful marble sculptures that fill the Chapel of San Severo in contrast to the reality of the landless peasants of the kingdom, and after a series of famines in the mid-1700s, tens of thousands of hungry peasants followed their grain to the capital. The number of urban poor swelled, and it was difficult for the city to accommodate them.

Meanwhile young men on the Grand Tour came to Napoli to experience Pompeii, but were certain before their first meal that the food they would eat in Napoli would be disgusting. This was a hard starting position for positive reviews of Napolitano cuisine. Travelers left with stereotyped impressions that came to shape the representation of the city to outsiders. Particularly striking to these privileged travelers were the large numbers of poor in the "low city," part of which is now the historic district and UNESCO World Heritage Site. The poor ate pizza and *maccheroni* because both were cheap foods in the early 1800s, and this did little to cultivate positive PR for Napoli's food culture. Durum wheat was an important ingredient to feed the growing numbers of poor in the kingdom's capital. *Maccheroni* production had been revolutionized with the introduction of screw presses that squeezed dough through perforated presses to make *maccheroni*. The near industrial scale of production made dried pasta very cheap, and generated huge demand for durum wheat from the rest of the kingdom. Napoli became the capital of dried pasta production, which along with pizza, became woven into the city's identity.

Because of desperate conditions in the poor neighbourhoods--crowding, malnutrition and non-existent sanitation--Napoli became associated with cholera in the 19th century, leading many tourists to steer clear of Europe's poorest city. While the cholera outbreaks of the late 1800s highlighted the dire reality of southern Italy in the newly unified nation, it also reminds us of the circumstances that encouraged large numbers of southern Italians to emigrate to the Americas, taking their food traditions with them.

In 1884, when a fresh wave of cholera washed over the city, there was a mass exodus of the upper classes. Everyone who could leave, did. The poor had nowhere to go, and more than 7,000 people died in one month. King Umberto visited the devastated city and declared that the city must be "disemboweled." This led to gentrification projects like demolishing tenements and building the wide Corso Umberto, a boulevard that cuts straight through the area most ravaged by cholera. When the king returned in 1889 to attend the official ceremonies associated with the completion of these projects, his wife Queen Margherita joined him. A local *pizzaiolo* (pizza maker) apparently sent three different types of pizza to the royals, and when the queen sent a letter indicating her favourite pizza, it was named pizza Margherita in her honour. This pizza, inspired by the colours of the new Italian flag (red tomatoes, green basil, and white buffalo mozzarella) became synonymous with Napoli. John Dicke argues that bestowing the queen's name on this poverty food was a way to dignify the poorest dish in the poorest city in Italy. The grit of Napoli today reminds me of this not-so-distant past, and that Napoli remains one of the poorest cities in the country (indeed in all of Europe).

The word *pizza* is related to the Greek word *pita*, and shares similarities with broader Mediterranean flatbreads. According to a description by the 16th century chef Bartolemeo Scappi, pizza at that time was a rich pie with marzipan crust filled with mashed almonds, pine nuts, dates, figs, raisins, and biscuits (a far cry from our modern version of a pizza pie). The early evolution of pizza and the use of the word is a bit unclear, but by the early 1800s, pizza in Napoli more closely resembled its modern form: bread dough in a round, with toppings that included different kinds of lard, cheese, tomatoes, and small fish.

My hands-on introduction to Neapolitan pizza came courtesy of Ciro Oliva. His busy pizzeria in the Rione Sanità quarter of Napoli was humming with all manner of prep work when we arrived to learn about this iconic food. For Ciro, pizza is about more than the stereotypes. He is very passionate about pizza. He cannot contain his enthusiasm as he talks about it, making it hard to squeeze in time for translation. His great-grandmother started her pizzeria in 1948 out of her home, keeping the front door open to be accessible from the street (still a common practice in southern Italian urban living). In a nod to the intimacy of neighbours, she practiced the idea of eating today and paying for it in eight days (something that you can do only if you have a relationship of trust with your customers). In his mid-twenties, as a fourth generation *pizzaiolo*, Ciro wants to do more than just sling pizza. He wants to maintain his family tradition and the idea of pizza as an identity that brings together the ingredients of history, culture, and local food products.

Pizzas are made here much as they have been for the last sixty-five years. At the front of the restaurant the *pizzaiolo* shapes the dough by hand, making the dough disk thinner in the centre and thicker in the outer part (where Americans expect a crust). Ingredients are sparingly spread on top, and then the pizza is put on the peel and quickly slid into the 450 degree Celsius wood-fired oven. The pizza will be completely cooked in 50 seconds. The guy running the peel is so confident that he doesn't need a timer. I didn't believe him so used my stopwatch: he popped a pizza onto the hot bricks inside the oven, turned it once, and pulled it out…in 47 seconds.

The next chapter in the story of Neapolitan pizza is its meteoric rise to iconic food stardom. Despite humble origins, in 2009, at Italy's request, *pizza napoletana* was safeguarded in the European Union as a Traditional Specialty Guaranteed dish. This means that its authenticity is not tied to one geographic place, like Altamura bread, but requires that it be made with San Marzano tomatoes and *mozzarella di bufala Campana* from the milk of water buffalo raised in the marshlands of Campania and Lazio (which itself is protected with its own European designation of origin). It must also be cooked in a very hot, wood-fired oven.

In 2016, Italians rejoiced with the successful bid to nominate pizza as an expression of cultural heritage. Nominations from around the globe are voted on by UNESCO every year, and the hope is that pizza will join the nearly four hundred other expressions of intangible culture that have been inscribed in an effort to raise awareness and protect these important cultural traditions. Ciro argues that everyone uses their own recipes, so Neapolitan pizza is a style rather than a single, stagnant recipe. Interestingly, many argue that this is meant to distinguish "real" pizza from North American impostors like New York pizza and, as often happens, reaction in North America has been swift and defensive. Are Italians trying to slap copyright protection on their iconic version of embellished flat bread, or simply trying proudly to own a very recognizable symbol of their identity? It remains to be seen. However, it is an interesting development in the story of pizza, where its poor, degraded beginnings have been conveniently forgotten in the zeal of nationalist pride.

These humble beginnings have not been completely forgotten though. Considering the history of pizza, it is perhaps fitting that Concettina ai Tre Santi is located in a neighbourhood considered by many to be a symbol of the poorest, most degraded character of Napoli. As you walk up the streets north of the busy Via Fornia, past the Palazzo San Felice, you can tell that while this neighbourhood may have been established for Napoli's aristocrats in the 1700s, its glory has been tarnished over the years due to unemployment, poverty, and the presence of the often feuding, Mafia-style Camorra clans that have resided here for centuries. Life spills into the streets. Produce stands, pedestrians, and scooters vie for space on the narrow roads. Store owners stand in front of their *tripperia* shops. Garbage collects in the gutters. Today, petty crime like pickpocketing is epidemic. This was the only place in the city where we were told that you risked losing a camera that was in plain sight rather than stashed in a bag. Over the years many volunteer and humanitarian efforts have focused on the Rione Sanità neighbourhood to address these issues, and Ciro wants to use food to build something more positive here, tapping into the social aspects of pizza. His socially-conscious business aims to give an identity and perspective to youth that are vulnerable to falling into petty crime.

Napoli has long been known for "suspended coffee" (*caffè sospeso*), whereby someone with some extra money and good fortune will pay for two coffees in one of the many working-class coffee bars in Napoli but only consume one. Later on, the second is given to someone in need. Concettina ai Tre Santi has adapted this concept of kindness and social responsibility to pizza: patrons can buy a "suspended pizza" the size of a large dinner plate (about 30cm in diameter) for 3 euros, and these pizzas are collected to support periodic social events. For example, in two months the pizzeria collected more than 700 pizzas to be cooked at an event. Ciro works with a foundation that focuses on education for children. He was proud to describe an upcoming event where the pizzeria, in partnership with a Michelin star chef, will have fun teaching children how to make pizza and encourage them to dream up new pizzas using local ingredients. One such creation from a previous event has made its way onto the pizzeria's menu and is named in honour of the foundation (see recipe below). At a time when there is so much focus on conserving European food identity with the likes of UNESCO designations, it is exciting to see a dynamic, modern identity expressed through food. This is a platform for Ciro to promote his pizza, his passion, and his message. He aims to elevate pizza in new ways, to new heights, and have local children connect with this food in meaningful ways. He celebrates a new take on old traditions, which maintains the social relevance of a food that has meant so many things over its history.

Concettina ai Tre Santi Pizza

There are four ingredients for Ciro's pizza dough--water, salt, yeast, flour--which makes this recipe deceptively easy. This recipe is dynamic and based on context; quantities may change subtly in response to the weather and the season. Napoli's hard water gives the dough an element that is not easily replicated elsewhere. Be prepared to experiment to define your dough for yourself!

1L water
1.65 kg flour (this is an equal parts mixture of three grades of flour, see the note below)
35g salt
0.1g brewer's yeast (BUT, as a testament to this "living" recipe, the amount of yeast is dependent on the temperature. Ciro checks every day and is trying to build a table to make the amount a bit more standardized in the business...when it's over 30 degrees C outside it's 0.1g but it can be anywhere up to 1g, so the average is going to be ½ tsp.)

Do NOT put olive oil in your dough. According to Ciro, "putting olive oil in the dough is just crazy!"

Ciro mixes 00 (very fine and refined, soft), 0 (fine, medium) and 1 (hard durum wheat) grade flours for his dough. This grading system indicates how finely the flour has been ground and how much bran and germ has been removed.

Low Protein + Low Starch + Low Gluten = soft flour – **00 flour or high grade flour**
High Protein +High Starch + High Gluten = hard flour – **hard durum wheat (semolina) flour or standard flour (1 grade)**

Most flour in North America is not labelled this way. To really try to replicate this recipe, you can hunt down Italian flour at specialty stores.

Directions:
Mix the flour into the water by hand. Add the salt, and once it is mixed in, add the dry yeast. Continue to mix and squeeze the dough by hand. The mixture is wet and sticky, and while there is a lot of kneading, Ciro calls it done long before a North American would. Expect the dough to still be sticky and soft rather than dry and hard.

The dough rises for 12-24 hours. It should rise on a wood board because the water from the dough is absorbed by the board. Rising happens in two steps. First, it rises as a whole ball for 6 hours. Second, it is cut and rolled into individual baseball-sized balls and allowed to rise for the balance of time. (The recipe yields 20 balls for personal pizzas.) The rising creates soft, airy dough that is ready to be shaped, dressed, and popped in the oven.

When it is time to make the pizza, the soft, elastic ball of dough is worked flatand stretched a little bit in all directions. The disk is flipped over several times to get it thinner. Then, it's a motion with your fingers to finish preparing the crust, a downward pressure using the entire finger, not just the tips to finish preparing the crust. Ciro would encourage you to dream up your own topping combinations, but if you want to emulate a Neapolitan pizza go easy on the toppings. The goal is not to homogenize the pizza so that every bit is the same; some bites will have more cheese than others, some will have a hit of basil. Remember that only pizzas with thin crusts and sparse toppings can cook in about a minute. Here are a few pizzas on the Concettina ai Tre Santi menu for inspiration:

Pizza Margherita

The most basic pizza is topped with tomato sauce, garlic, basil, oregano, buffalo mozzarella or *fiori di latte* (fresh mozzarella made from cow's milk). As a symbol of nationalism it sports the colours of the Italian flag.

Pizza Fondazione di San Gennaro

First, line the exterior of the circle of dough with thin, matchstick-sized pieces of salami and provolone cheese. Then roll over to create a stuffed crust. Next, spread tomato sauce in the middle, plus basil leaves, and more provolone cheese but less than in North America. After it's cooked, crumble almond *taralli* (savory crisp bread rings, almost like a crouton in this context) over top. This one was developed by kids at one of the suspended pizza events, and so is called Fondazione di San Gennaro.

Pizzas should be flash cooked in a very hot oven. Unless you are cooking in a wood-fired oven it is hard to get temperatures of 450 degrees Celsius. Try a 500 degree Fahrenheit oven and watch the pizza carefully. The toppings should bubble and brown but not burn. You want the crust to be cooked but not crisp on the bottom.

In Napoli, in a perplexing reversal of etiquette, the food that was once considered unhygienic because, as street food, it was eaten with the hands while walking, is eaten with a fork and knife, not your hands.

7. Tomatoes: A "despised" and "dangerous" fruit?

The poor tomato: misunderstood, relegated to the unfortunate who had few other choices when it came to food. Domesticated in central America thousands of years ago and brought to Spain in the early 16th century by returning Spanish conquistadors, the tomato, like many other introductions from the "New World," was eyed with suspicion. Europeans had a hard time fitting these foreign items into their existing food systems. Some things were considered curiosities, or medicines, or merely animal feed (as with corn in central Europe), influencing their more mainstream introduction and incorporation into food traditions. But the tomato was labelled poisonous, and the fears and rumours of the plant's lethal properties were hard to shake.

The various European names for the tomato are evidence of its origins and then spread across Europe. In Nahuatl, the Aztec language, the fruit was called *tomatl*, which was liberally borrowed by the Spanish with little modification ("tomato" in Spanish is *tomate*). As the tomato spread through Europe, it is possible that because it was introduced alongside the eggplant, which the French called *pomme des Mours* ("fruit of the Moors") because it was favoured in Arab cuisine, it was mispronounced *pomme d'amour* in France and in turn became *pomodoro* in Italy. What is more probable though is that the similarities between the tomato and the mandrake, called *dudaim* in Hebrew, which translates roughly into "love apple," were noted early on, leaving its mark on the name of this new fruit. This demystifies the Italian translation "golden apple" for a fruit that is predominantly red in Europe. Indeed, in Britain, tomatoes were originally called "love apples" and grown ornamentally in gardens long before they were eaten.

The tomato's biggest problem was its guilt by association. Tomatoes are part of the Solanaceae family, which includes deadly nightshades and other poisonous plants like the mandrake that contain toxins called tropane alkaloids. The much-feared mandrake was called a "love apple" because of its reference in the Book of Genesis as an aphrodisiac. Thanks to the likes of Italian herbalist Pietro Andrea Mattioli, who made the early connections between the foreign tomato and the familiar (and somewhat terrifying) Mediterranean mandrake, the tomato acquired a reputation for being both poisonous *and* a source of temptation. Its luscious red complexion, juicy disposition, and zesty flavour just added to the prevailing view that the tomato inflamed passions in dangerous and "un-Christian" ways. Plus, tomatoes have many seeds, adding to its reputation as an aphrodisiac. In the 16th century it was widely believed that a food's qualities would influence those who consumed it, so eating something with lots of seeds presumably increased fertility and virility.

A story with no real supporting evidence is that aristocrats brave enough to try this new exotic food appeared to get sick and die after eating them, seemingly reinforcing all suggestions of the tomato's poisonous qualities. The reality though is that the tomato was an innocent bystander. Many European aristocrats used pewter plates, which were high in lead content. When tomatoes, which are quite acidic, were placed on pewter plates, the acid would leach the lead from the plate, leading to poisoning and death. Since lead poisoning is a slow process that accumulates over time it is hard to believe that tomatoes could have done this kind of harm, both to humans and to the valuable pewter dishes, let alone that people could have made a connection between this type of poisoning and tomatoes. A more compelling reason for being considered poisonous may be due to a weird chemical reaction that takes place when tomatoes (and other very acidic foods) are consumed with wine: the wine tastes bad. As Renata Kestryl has noted, this sudden change in the taste of wine would make people weary of the new ingredient.

Another interesting obstacle in the adoption of the tomato was the prevailing medical paradigm of humorism, whereby the qualities of hot, cold, wet and dry had to be carefully balanced to ensure optimal health. Even spices, which were nearly all considered "hot" and "dry", could not fully balance juicy tomatoes (especially raw ones), that were considered moist in the 4th (potentially deadly) degree, making them a supremely unhealthy food.

(Cooked tomato sauce helped the tomato make culinary inroads, especially paired with chicken as in dishes like chicken *cacciatore*, because cooking made them warmer and they were a good counter balance to "dry" chicken.)

Terrible, horrible, despised: what to make of this acidic fruit dangerously associated with both love and death? John Gerard summed up the sentiment of the time in his widely read herbal publication in 1597: tomatoes were poisonous and *"of ranke and stinking savour."* Others cautioned that eating tomatoes would make your teeth fall out; indeed, just the smell of them was thought to drive people insane! It seems obvious that most steered clear of tomatoes in favour of other choices. One wonders how tomatoes made any inroads at all in European cuisine given the prejudice! Due to their exotic origin, tomatoes would have been initially most available to the European elite; their popularity in these circles took quite a long time to develop. If cookbooks are a good indicator of culinary developments in the literate upper classes, tomatoes are present very sparingly in European cookbooks of the late 1500s. At this time it seems that the tomato may have been eaten more by the southern poor, whose lack of food choice led to bravely trying tomatoes, and the recognition that they did not deserve their despised reputation.

A street vendor in Napoli advertises fresh Piccadilly tomatoes. This variety can be hung and preserved without refrigeration for several weeks.

The first tomato sauce recipes come from Napoli, and date to the 1690s, nearly 150 years after tomatoes first reached the Spanish territories of the southern Italian peninsula. The recipes provide some guidance on what you can do with tomatoes, and promote the Spanish form of use (*"alla Spagnuola"*). The first evidence of a tomato sauce specifically for pasta appears in a Neapolitan cookbook in 1844, and may be the ancestor to "marinara sauce," now a prerequisite for spaghetti in Italian-American cuisine. John Mariani explains how the sauce was named in his book *How Italian Food Conquered the World*: "There was a simple one of garlic, oil, and tomatoes called marinara, supposedly because it was made quickly, as soon as the mariners' wives spotted their husbands' fishing boats returning in the distance." At around the same time, tomato sauce was spread on pizza dough rounds, and Napoli's iconic food was born!

It wasn't until the late 1800s that tomato sauce spread much beyond Napoli to every corner of Italy, thanks in great part to new canning techniques that liberated cooks from using only fresh tomatoes (which were restricted both geographically and seasonally). Today the tomato is a celebrated part of the Mediterranean diet. The antioxidant lycopene found in tomatoes has recently been linked to many health benefits, including reducing the risk of heart disease and some cancers.

Rotten tomatoes: tomato economics in a modern world

Today, tomatoes remain dangerous only to the people who pick them in southern Italy. The demand for canned tomatoes and various forms of sauces and concentrates has shaped the modern agricultural economies of southern Italy. Statistics from 2010 indicate that the tomato industry is worth $2.2 billion (USD) annually. The 6.6 million tons of tomatoes are picked by thousands of workers every year, and increasingly the agricultural sector is relying on large numbers of migrants who have escaped war and poverty and come to Italy hoping for a better life. This dream is rarely realized.

There is a long tradition of exploitation in the agricultural system of southern Italy. In the feudal system, hired farm workers, the *braccianti* (from *braccia*, meaning arms), were the poorest category of labourer. This was because they did not own land and could not lease it because they were poor. They were hired for occasional labour but that was not reliable employment. Despite their lowly position, the system depended on the *braccianti* as a large pool of cheap labour, which became more important as the Industrial Revolution ushered in new competitive pressures from the developing global market.

Today, migrant agricultural workers are the equivalent of the *braccianti*. Migrant workers arrive in Puglia in the early summer as part of their "seasonal workers trek," where they follow the picking work around southern Italy based on the seasonality of different produce. Workers are asylum seekers, refugees, and economic migrants (the majority are men from sub-Saharan Africa). In 2005, Doctors Without Borders found that more than half those interviewed did not have any kind of valid permit. Because they are vital to the agricultural sector, authorities tolerate illegal workers, but this makes them vulnerable to abuse. Stories emerged of physically abusive discipline and foremen tipping off police to illegal immigrants just before payday.

Without contracts from employers they are invisible and have very few rights.

Since 2005, journalists and Doctors Without Borders have exposed the undignified, inhumane conditions endured by thousands of men and women who pick the tomatoes that are shipped to factories in Napoli, Salerno, and Caserta to be made into *passata* and concentrate. It is piece work, with pickers being paid 3 euros per crate that, when full, weighs 300 kilograms (660 pounds). Pickers are generally filling three to four of these crates per day to make a meager wage, and work days are 10-14 hours long. The brokers and harvest managers, called *caporali*, who find individuals work often take a cut of daily wages, leaving next to nothing at the end of the day. Contractual "irregularities" are common, leading to extreme vulnerability. Local priest Father Arcangelo Maira in trying to help immigrants told Reuters in 2009, *"It's a feudal system like in the Middle Ages. These modern slaves are handy for the economy: you can exploit them and then get rid of them when you don't need them anymore."*

A great many workers crawl home at the end of the day to ghetto style accommodation, often much worse than what they left behind in their home countries. Shacks and abandoned buildings become the homes of thousands of foreign labourers who arrive for the picking season, which generally runs from August to October. Makeshift camps of cardboard shacks house hundreds more workers. Only recently have authorities provided portable toilets. The MSF report found workers living in overcrowded conditions with inadequate toilet facilities. (In one instance there were one hundred people living in a building with only two toilets.)

The 2005 MSF report was an exposé of the dirty underbelly of this industry, but it doesn't seem to have made much of a difference. In 2012, Amnesty International published a report that highlighted the same allegations of abuse. What fuels this widespread labour exploitation is price, and over the last 25 years the price has only gone down. There are even cheap Chinese tomatoes that are now processed in Italy and then sold as Italian tomatoes. Many farmers have not been able to make money farming tomatoes so have stopped, but for the others to compete, and be able to produce a jar of tomato sauce for 1.50 euro per kilogram, they nip and tuck both in terms of human welfare and the environment.

The chronic exploitation in the fields has fuelled the efforts of a small start-up business called Funky Tomato. It is an operation consciously designed to create a supply chain free from exploitation of humans or the planet, an alternative to illegal hiring, ghetto-style living, and slave-like conditions for the sake of cheap food. Italy is awash in immigrants and refugees, and sees them as a tremendous burden that will require endless handouts. Funky Tomato wants to redefine immigrants as a tremendous resource who have the potential to enrich the culture of southern Italy. Even the name--Funky Tomato--is a nod to the funk music scene, which celebrates the fusion of soul music, jazz, and R&B to create a novel form of music that at its inception represented the realities of the modern world for African-Americans and was an outlet for social commentary about racial oppression, violence, and broken dreams.

Unlike the piecework of the mainstream tomato industry, Funky Tomato guarantees an hourly wage of 8 euros, plus some benefits. Pickers generally work about 6-8 hours per day, and pick about 400 pounds per person. It doesn't take a math genius to see the difference; industry pickers must work faster, harder, and longer hours than the mostly West African migrant workers that are hired by Funky Tomato. In Italy workers must put in at least 52 working days to earn the agricultural unemployment benefit. Funky Tomato meets this goal, and offers seasonal contracts to labourers of 39 hours per week. At the height of the picking season, Funky Tomato has been able to employ thirty people. The tomato fields that Funky Tomato manages are also non-intensive and organic; seed varieties are chosen that work well in the hot, arid environment which means they need less water but don't produce as much per plant. Funky Tomato plants produce 1.5-2 kilograms per plant, significantly less than the industry standard of 6-7 kilograms per plant. It is obvious that there is a price (both in terms of picking efficiency and yield) for more environmentally sensitive agriculture.

The Funky Tomato project was launched with the support of prospective customers who pre-paid for 20,000 jars of preserved tomatoes and sauce. The hope is that that this renewed focus on quality and ethical production will resonate with like-minded businesses willing to pay a bit more for tomatoes. (And it's not too hard to put your money where your mouth is: Funky Tomato sells its 600g jar for 1.70 euros, only 20 cents more than the mainstream industry.) By reconnecting with the landscape and with humans, both producers and consumers, Funky Tomato hopes to build a sustainable business in the midst of Italy's gigantic tomato industry and improve the image of this storied fruit in new ways.

8. Olives and "Liquid Gold"

The whole Mediterranean, the sculpture, the palms, the gold breads, the bearded heroes, the wine, the ideas, the ships, the moonlight, the winged gorgons, the bronze men, the philosophers--all of it seems to rise in the sour, pungent smell of these black olives between the teeth. A taste older than meat, older than wine. A taste as...old as cold water.
-Lawrence Durrell

Thousands of tiny white flowers in May are the promise of a great harvest in late fall, assuming that the weather or the olive fly or some other blight does not serious damage the crop. A 10-15% loss is considered a good year, and the only consolation is that the ruined olives return to the soil as fertilizer for next year's fruit.

Olive oil is the only oil that is extracted from a fruit (other than coconut). Olives have been processed for a long time (a 10,000 year old olive press has been found in Turkey), and the oil has been used as the base for perfumes, lamps, rituals, and food. Greek athletes used to slather themselves with oil before wrestling, making their skin aesthetically shiny and functionally slippery. Olive oil lamps lit the rise of the great Greek, and later Roman states, and the oil was critical to the Roman Empire's economy. Ships with holds full of ceramic amphorae plied the Mediterranean from Spain to the Italian peninsula to supply the intense demand for the product. At one point records indicate that people in Rome used two litres of oil per month. Because returning empty containers to the provinces and reusing them did not make good financial sense, the containers were smashed and dumped in what is now Mount Testaccio in Rome. The artificial hill, comprised of 580,000 cubic meters (760,000 cubic yards) of ceramic fragments, stands 35 meters high and represents over 50 million ceramic amphorae and 1.3 billion litres of oil! Olive oil has been an important symbol of health, religion, and wealth. The rich vegetable fat is a key ingredient in the celebrated Mediterranean diet. In southern Italy it is still considered a food rather than just a condiment, and is used liberally on everything, even toast.

In mid-November, Puglia's olive groves are humming with activity. Carefully pruned and tended, the trees are heavy with fruit that is ready to be picked and quickly whisked away to the mill, where the fruit undergoes a transformation from small hard globe to what the Romans called liquid gold. Nets are stretched under trees so that the fruit is not bruised as it is shaken from the branches; this is also a reason why the fruit is harvested before it is perfectly ripe, and when there is the highest level of antioxidants that impart a peppery aftertaste to the oil. As an unsaturated fat, the high quality of olive oil begins to degrade almost as soon as the olives are picked, so a day's yield is pressed within hours at communal presses.

Crates of freshly picked olives are taken to the communal press every day, where they are labelled and pressed so that each farmer knows he is getting his own oil back.

Bottled in dark glass or in large tins to minimize exposure to light, good olive oil will last for eighteen months to two years. Inferior quality oils, the olive oil that the majority of North Americans have become accustomed to in price and taste, does not have the same quantities of beneficial antioxidants that offer excellent health benefits to consumers but also protect the oil itself from spoiling quickly. North Americans are very familiar with a nutty flavour rather than a peppery one in their oil, which is a telltale sign that the oil has gone rancid.

Because of the increasing geographic and psychological distance between olive grove and kitchen, consumers are at the mercy of cunning marketing techniques when it comes to olive oil. The farther away from the olive tree, the harder it is to trace the origins and evaluate the integrity of the oil--and the companies selling it. There are many words that are used to market olive oil and that appear to distinguish one product from the next and play with romantic imagery to sway consumers. Evaluating these terms helps to understand the process of oil extraction and the maze of advertising.

"Extra virgin" is a term that appeared in the 1970s. It is based on Italian legislation from the previous decade that offered definitions and subsequent classifications, and is associated with a new system of extraction. Traditionally, stone mills crushed olives and the paste was put on a flax cloth that was then pressed with either a screw or lever. The juice came out and was collected, after which the oil and water would separate and the oil could be skimmed off the top. Newer technology involves a centrifuge process that avoids exposure to the air and thus contamination. One problem with the new technology is that you lose a lot of the flavour because of the heat involved in the process. In contrast, the traditional system is cold pressed but exposes the oil to bacterial attack. A new cooling system has been developed to address this issue, hence the term "cold extracted," but really everything is cold pressed so it's just a charade.

The olives are only ever pressed once to extract oil, so there is no "second press" oil, making "first press" another fine example of marketing. However, there is still about 5-10 percent of the oil left in the mash after the first press, which can be considered lost profit, so a new system sends the mash to a refinery (also referred to as a pomace oil extraction facility) where hexane is used to chemically extract the rest of the oil. As you drive through Puglia you can smell these refineries long before you see them, producing oil that is used for things like soap or cheap grade food oil that may simply be called "olive oil" for unsuspecting consumers. The oil may be coloured to make it more "authentic" green, deodorized, and transformed into a bland lifeless product that will do little more than make sure your vegetables don't stick to the bottom of the pan.

The terms *virgin* and *extra virgin* relate to the oil's acidity level. Extra virgin olive oil must have an acidity of between 0.2 to 0.8 percent, while oil with 0.8 to 2 percent acidity can legally be called virgin. Anything more acidic is not good for eating, but is sometimes refined further to make it fit for consumption. The resulting oil is quite tasteless and colourless, hence its name "light oil," although some consumers may think it is a diet product.

Olive trees can live for thousands of years. Maybe the fact that individuals can harvest olives from the same trees that their great-great-grandparents harvested contributes to the tremendous sense of identity that is tied to olives. In the last few years a new blight has sent shockwaves through European olive groves, and the knee-jerk reaction to this terror is to advocate cutting the groves to the ground. This is a devastating proposition for the living heritage that these trees represent.

Less expensive (and sometimes morally corrupt) brands have also been accused of shipping olive oil and other cheaper oils like hazelnut, canola, and sunflower oils from areas with less expensive production costs to Italy, where it is bottled and then exported as 100 percent Italian extra virgin olive oil. Somehow this is allowed, and this fraudulent oil undercuts the competition. It's worth noting that these shady practices are common in all olive-producing countries, generating a significant challenge for consumers, be it low quality oil palmed off as "extra virgin," or mixtures of cheap vegetable oils with green dye and questionable provenance. Forbes magazine recently reported that upwards of 80 percent of olive oil gracing grocery store shelves is not what it is reported to be on the label.

How can this be avoided? How can we source good, true olive oil? Supporting small producers is key. Recently there has been a trend that is seeing new, small, young producers going back to farming and a rural lifestyle while adopting new technology and striving for top quality. The most successful of these producers are those who can connect with consumers along a short production chain, similar to the merits of Fairtrade that cuts out middlemen and encourages fair prices for product. It is by building these relationships of trust that both the new generation of producers and informed consumers can get what they want and need. As consumers though we will have to recalibrate our expectations when it comes to price. Real, good quality olive oil--not coloured, blended oil that is marketed as olive oil--represents a huge amount of work for the return. Although olive trees can be harvested after two years, young trees do not produce huge amounts of oil. Tonio Creanza's family olive grove of 700 trees, which includes some that are 400 years old, produces 1200-1400 litres of oil per season (each tree produces 1.5 to 2 litres of oil per year). Creanza Family olive oil is about four times as expensive as large commercial brands, a reflection of the huge amount of labour involved in harvesting olives that keeps families very busy in the month of November.

Get ready: real olive oil, the stuff with the health benefits of the Mediterranean diet packs a peppery punch. This pronounced flavour (especially when tasted properly) indicates the presence of polyphenyls, the beneficial antioxidants that contribute to the health allure of the Mediterranean diet. Research now links regular olive oil consumption to a healthier heart, a lower incidence of some forms of cancer (including breast cancer and skin cancer) and a lower risk of Type II diabetes. It reduces inflammation, positively affects bone density in fighting osteoporosis, and while preliminary, research indicates that it may significantly lower the risk of strokes. Olive oil also seems to have a protective function against dementia and Alzheimer's disease. Interestingly, the island of Sardinia has a considerable concentration of people who live to be over one hundred years old, and in her book *Olive Odyssey* Julie Angus suggests that the daily habit of consuming two tablespoons of olive oil may have something to do with this! In a culture obsessed with delaying the effects of aging, extra virgin olive oil seems to be what fills the Holy Grail. Keep in mind though that these health benefits don't come from cheap, "fake" oil, and once you have tasted full-flavoured extra virgin olive oil it is difficult to use cheap olive oil as a salad dressing!

Olives and "liquid gold"

9. Pastoralism: Shepherding through the ages

I could hear them before I could see them. I had just stepped out of an old shepherd's house as we awaited milk to warm up and be magically transformed into cheese, and I heard the tinny sound of bells. As I watched, they appeared over the hill across from us, a tight bundle of white sheep kept together by a lone black and white sheepdog who was being guided by a shepherd. They slowly moved down the slope, flowing over the low stone walls like an advancing wave. When they reached the area in front of where we stood the dog expertly conducted the sheep around us like a tornado. This was the closest I had ever got to the source of cheese, and I was mesmerized. In southern Italy, pastoralism is a good way to win food from a rocky limestone landscape that can only be farmed in pockets where fertile soil has developed. For millennia wheat agriculture and pastoralism have been woven together across the landscape, the farmers maximizing the yield of fields punctuated by high points of exposed, rocky limestone that are better suited for grazing sheep. Watch sheep grazing and you will start to understand how food and the people who produce and consume it are shaped by their surroundings!

Out in the fields, with swallows diving about eating bugs, clouds racing across a blue sky, and wind leisurely caressing the tall grasses, it felt like a world away from my urban reality in so many ways. The lifestyle of shepherds is unfamiliar to most North Americans today. The sight of sheep being herded along a country road conjures images of hard working, self-sacrificing shepherds and romantic feelings of authentic, rural landscapes untouched by the advances of modernity. In a similar way, pastoralism lends its name to a genre of literature, art and music called "pastorals" that depicts such life in an idealized manner, typically for urban audiences. Although the roots of this genre may be much older, its popularity surged during the Renaissance in Europe and Britain. Perhaps it is no coincidence that this is when urban centres began to expand and the foundations of the Industrial Revolution were laid, and when the relationships between rural and urban, and humans and nature began their most dramatic transformations. Written by members of the urban middle class, pastorals are a great example of "othering," where representation is created by an outsider.

In pastorals, the pastoral life is usually characterized as being closer to the Golden Age than the rest of human life. Created in opposition to the urban life, the shepherd appears as a virtuous soul because of his humble relationship with nature, uncorrupted by the temptations of the city. The genre channels a sense of nostalgia for a romanticized, ideal pastoral life that has been lost. The urban centre, and more recently and more broadly Industrialism, has distanced consumers from producers. Surrounded by the noisy, fast-paced life of modernity, city dwellers cast a longing glance back to a peaceful, stress-free life that we once had in the countryside. A Paradise Lost.

What I have come to understand is that the life of a shepherd may have a different tempo from city life, but it is by no means stress free and idyllic, and never has been. The Bible is an interesting place to learn about shepherds, and can provide some time depth in assessing the changing value of shepherds and their products. At the time of Christ, shepherds in the Levant had really fallen off the social ladder and were caught in a changing social reality that valued crops more than dairy and meat. They smelled like sheep. They slept on the ground. They didn't live in major cities. Their jobs made them little or no money. This is actually not so different from the modern reality of shepherds, and reminds us of the requirements of shepherding that continue to include measures of sacrifice.

Pastoral imagery in Christianity

Sheep, goats, and shepherds feature prominently in Christianity. This pastoral imagery reflects history, and ancient subsistence traditions that are far removed from the dominant North American reality today but would have been very familiar in the ancient Mediterranean world at the inception and spread of the Abrahamic religions. That Christian priests continue to be called pastors (Latin for "shepherd"), that the Anglican bishop's staff looks like a shepherd's crook, and that the Lord's Prayer reminds us that "the Lord is my shepherd" may be the extent to which we associate pastoralism with Christianity. The pastoral metaphor is much richer and more complex though, and it can provide some historic context to help us understand the changing values of both shepherd and sheep.

The Ancient Israelites, occupying the arid, sandy landscape of the Levant, were a pastoral people and shepherding was a noble occupation. In nomadic societies, everyone, regardless of social position, was a shepherd. Many biblical figures were shepherds, among them the patriarchs Abraham and Jacob, the prophet Moses, and King David. Their flocks were sizable. For example, Job reportedly had 14,000 sheep and King Solomon sacrificed 120,000 sheep at the dedication of the Temple. When the twelve tribes of Israel migrated to Egypt, they encountered a lifestyle foreign to them. The Egyptians were farmers, and there was tension between farmers and shepherds because of competing land use. Neighbouring Arabs were shepherds. Battles between agriculturalists and shepherds were common. Indeed, the first recorded murder in Western history erupted from a farmer's resentment of a shepherd (Genesis 4:1-8) because God preferred the gift of Abel, keeper of the sheep, over that of Cain, tiller of the field. One can understand this tension in terms of landscape use, but consider it in terms of religious message: shepherds always look like they are basking in God's good favour. With the ability to adapt more flexibly to changing environmental conditions, their efforts lead to wealth (sheep) while a farmer can toil away and then experience a drought, which is cruel evidence that God is not satisfied. No wonder the shepherd could seem like God's favourite, thus sowing the seeds of resentment.

In the course of four hundred years the Israelites' perception of shepherding slowly changed, and after settling in Palestine, shepherding started to lose its prominent position. After carrying the Ark as a mobile religious artifact, Judaism settled into the Temple, a sign of more settled populations tethered to fields and crops. These new social structures were incompatible with the wanderings of shepherds. Agriculture increased, and pasturage decreased, confined to marginal areas in the wilderness of Judea and Bethlehem. As a labouring class, shepherds were now considered second-class citizens and untrustworthy. They shared the same unenviable status as tax collectors and dung sweepers. They could not fulfill judicial offices or be admitted in court as witnesses. While sheep were important forms of sacrifice, and were valued as sources of food and wool, their keepers were not.

It is into this social context that Jesus stepped. How surprising and significant that God chose marginalized shepherds to be the first to hear the joyous news of the birth of Christ instead of a rabbi or dignitaries.

And in the same region there were shepherds out in the field, keeping watch over their flock by night. And an angel of the Lord appeared to them, and the glory of the Lord shone around them, and they were filled with fear. Luke 2:8-9

This was not a random encounter, the recipients of the angel's message were carefully chosen. The story helps paint a picture of the shepherd's reality in Palestine two thousand years ago. Working conditions of shepherds were challenging, which included tending their flocks on winter nights that would have been cool and wet, with rainfall increasing from December through February. Because of their isolation in the fields and the constant attention that their animals required, it was difficult for shepherds to observe organized religious practices, but in this particular case, the shepherds were engaged in important religious service. Early Jewish traditions recorded in the *Mishnah* indicate that the Messiah would be revealed from the tower of the flock, located close to Bethlehem. Shepherds looking after flocks in this location took care of the temple-flocks, the sheep meant for sacrifice. This audience seems appropriate to receive a divine message about the ultimate lamb who would take away the sins of the world through His death and resurrection.

The biblical Good Shepherd

Morals and social structures are commonly shared in story. And the most effective story, the one that keeps the audience's attention, is one that weaves metaphor into the story's fabric, easily understood by the audience because of shared social context. The shepherd metaphor helped present Christianity as something distinct from the Judaism of the time. Christ spent most of his life walking amongst the lowly, and his messages would have been very appealing to this audience, the marginalized who could appreciate the poignant metaphors of pastoralism. Much of the deep metaphor is lost on a modern audience unfamiliar with pastoralism and disconnected from food producers. As a result we have reduced the meaning to the most general; we are sheep to be herded by God and/or Jesus. However, to original audiences it is not so much a commentary about followers as sheep as it is a consideration of what makes a good shepherd. Psalm 23, in the Gospel of John (John 10:11-18), presents a powerful narrative of leadership, care, responsibility, and sacrifice:

I am the good shepherd. The good shepherd lays down his life for the sheep. He who is a hired hand, and not a shepherd, who doesn't own the sheep, sees the wolf coming, leaves the sheep, and flees. The wolf snatches the sheep, and scatters them. The hired hand flees because he is a hired hand, and doesn't care for the sheep. I am the good shepherd. I know my own, and I'm known by my own; even as the Father knows me, and I know the Father. I lay down my life for the sheep. I have other sheep, which are not of this fold. I must bring them also, and they will hear my voice. They will become one flock with one shepherd. Therefore the Father loves me, because I lay down my life, that I may take it again. No one takes it away from me, but I lay it down by myself. I have power to lay it down, and I have power to take it again. I received this commandment from my Father.

The foundation of the story offers a fascinating reflection of the everyday in texts commonly considered primarily for their religious content. Kenneth Bailey, a renowned Biblical scholar, suggests that each family in a village would have owned a couple of sheep for personal use. The animals lived at night in the family courtyard, and one individual would shepherd a combined flock of many families. One can imagine the sound in the morning as this shepherd made his way down the street gathering the sheep. This would have been a daily occurrence and profoundly familiar to the audience of John's story. Individuals would recognize their shepherd and open the door to the courtyard, letting the animals pass through. The sheep recognized a distinct call, whistle, or small flute used by their shepherd, and would follow him out of the village.

The role of sacrifice in pastoralism, both physically and metaphorically, can be recognized in a number of ways. Not only do shepherds forsake the comforts of family and home to look after the needs of their animals, but they put the needs of the animals above everything: *the good shepherd lays down his life for the sheep.* This is very effective in communicating the love and responsibility that Jesus sees in his role. Unlike a "minimum wage" tender of the flocks, who will run if a wolf shows up, Jesus argues that he will fight the wolf and even give his life for the sake of his sheep, reinforcing the noble qualities of a good shepherd. I wonder how this fits in a modern context, with shepherding once again devalued and increasingly relying on the hired hands of immigrant labourers to do the hard work that is required in the pastures of southern Italy.

Transhumance in southern Italy

Christianity was originally a pastoral tradition and so appealed to other pastoralists. It may well have spread through the pastoral landscape of the southern Mediterranean because of the common appeal of its metaphors; the infrastructure of tracks that were used by shepherds to move their flocks between pastures were also used by merchants, armies, and pilgrims. As early as the second millennium BC, this huge network of ancient shepherds' tracks covered thousands of kilometers and ultimately connected disparate regions from Spain to the Carpathians in Eastern Europe (and likely beyond into the Middle East). Many of these ancient tracks and grazing spaces became the foundation for the impressive infrastructure of the Roman Empire, with its

Sheep and goats meander along the tratturo that runs past the Fornello site outside of Altamura.

roads connecting strategic cities.

These tracks were used for the daily movements of animals, but also supported the practice of transhumance, a term that comes from the Latin "*trans*" (across) and "*humus*" (ground) and is applied to the seasonal migration of pastoralists and their animals. For at least the last 3,000 years the people of the Murgia Plateau and neighbouring mountainous territories in Abruzzo and Molise on the southern Italian peninsula have been shaped by the twin traditions and lifestyles of low-intensity farming and shepherding. Shepherding has been the basis of economy, social structure, and cultural tradition in these regions since pre-Roman times, and is an excellent adaptation to the arid climate and rocky, thin soils of the limestone plateau. At least one breed of sheep, the *Altamurana* variety, is a product of this landscape. While they do not produce as much milk as other varieties, they are hardy and do well in the bare, dry environments of the Murgia with its wild green natural pastures. This landscape supported a seasonal migration of sheep at the end of spring and again at the beginning of autumn, where shepherds used the network of paths and grazing corridors, called *tratturi*, to move their animals long distances between summer grazing areas in the Apennines in Abruzzo and winter grazing on the Murgia Plateau. In this region the *tratturi* were considered public grazing lands that were governed by agrarian laws first instituted by the Romans. While seasonal migrations stalled in the Middle Ages, there was a resurgence in the 10th and 11th centuries when the region became Europe's leading producer of wool and propelled the social, economic, and cultural development of the southern peninsula. By the 14th century, transhumance was a state-regulated system. Rest areas for shepherds and their animals, fences, shelters and holding pens, fountains, chapels, taverns, and inns had been erected along these tracks. Not

84

only did this maintain the viability of transhumance, it also supplied services to those using them (and created good places to collect taxes as a shepherd's fee for using these grazing paths). Alfonso I, King of Naples, established an office for the protection of the Royal Shepherds' Track in 1442, and subsequent laws called the *Dogana* protected the entire network of shepherds' paths in the kingdom. Infringement on these paths was subject to punishment by death and testifies to the value of the *tratturi*.

Legal protections helped to make shepherding the leading sector of the economy. But as history teaches us, this relationship between farmer and shepherd is a dynamic one, and things began to change in the 1600s. Across much of Europe, a combination of population increase and the influences of the Industrial Revolution led to a decline in pastoralism by the 18th century. The ancient tension between agriculture and sheep farming was in crisis. Nineteenth century laws designed to maximize the growing of crops tipped the scales in favour of farmers. Mussolini's "Battle of the Grain" in the 1930s explicitly valued agriculture over other subsistence uses, which was hard on shepherds. This economic policy was designed to make Italy self-sufficient in grain, and reduce the need for foreign imports of bread. Since farmers could get subsidies to buy machinery if they were growing wheat, it was predictable that the rural landscape shifted in favour of the plough. By the mid-20th century the pattern of transhumance had all but disappeared.

Perhaps because of the geology of the Murgia Plateau, and the limitations that the landscape placed on food producers, the symbiotic relationship between herder and farmer has persisted; shepherds herd their small flocks locally, either on their own land, leased land, or by the grace of their neighbours. Just as shepherds seemed to be out of sync with the reality of Christ's time, shepherds today are challenged by government policies that seem to be stacked against them, and a public wooed by the allure of cheap supermarket cheese who may forget the taste of true shepherding products.

A modern Good Shepherd

There is no better way to appreciate the deep metaphors of the Bible and the reality of modern shepherds in southern Italy than to spend a whole day with one. Giovanni Maino lives on a farm about ten kilometers south of Altamura, a farm that he has rented for over forty years and that his father used before him. Like many tenants, Giovanni has trouble convincing the landlord to put money into the property. The roof of the 13th century tower where he sleeps leaks, and he has recently taken it upon himself to update the small living space with a tile floor and indoor bathroom. The compound includes a small room partially built into the rock where he makes pecorino cheese and ricotta, and enclosures for his pigs, turkeys, and ducks. There is a large area for the sheep and goats, with a cave next to it that can be used to corral the animals at milking time, and sheds for chickens, rabbits, and a lone cow. Paired with a small food garden, this compound and the pastures behind it support Giovanni's family of ten. The eight children and his wife Elisa live in a house in town; Giovanni lives full time at the farm because the animals need constant care. This family split between town and country is very common for food producers here; Elisa comes to the farm every day, and the family visits on the weekends and school holidays. Having a car makes this divide much easier to navigate. Not so long ago shepherds were isolated in the countryside for weeks, coming in to town to visit the family and bring in milk and cheese to sell. The life of a shepherd continues to be one of absolute dedication to his animals; the sheep and goats dictate the rhythm of the shepherd's day.

The day starts at 6:00 am with the animals being milked. The flock of 280 animals (about half of which are goats and the rest sheep) are corralled in a big cave and squeeze by a fence that Giovanni and his son Alessio have set up to allow Giovanni to milk them as they pass by him. Because many have babies he doesn't milk each one, and some get milked for slightly longer than others. While one might assume that mechanization would be a real progressive advantage, Giovanni is incredibly efficient, milking each animal for only about ten seconds before the next one pushes in. He knows each animal, which ones are nursing young, which

Giovanni milks a goat as another impatiently waits at his right shoulder. Both goat and sheep's milk mingles in a large plastic bucket.

ones were milked more at the last milking, and he evaluates all of this as he works. Hand milking also maintains more of a connection with the animals to carefully evaluate their health: when their teats are slightly warmer this can be the first sign of an infection, which can then be quickly treated to keep the rest of the flock and the milk healthy.

The sun burns off the early morning fog, and the yard fills with animals as they are milked or leave the cave, impatient babies jumping over the backs of adults being milked. The milking is done by 7:00 am and then it is time to make cheese. Giovanni pulls out milk from the previous two and a half days, which had been kept cool in a cave next to the cheese-making space. Like his father before him Giovanni warms the milk in a cauldron over a fire rather than a gas burner. The blackened walls of the small room are testament to years of cheese making here. First up are rounds of pecorino. Amounts are not measured, and other than the use of a thermometer everything is done by feel. Once the milk is heated the rennet needs time to work its magic, which gives us time for a quick coffee. When we return at 7:30 am the curd has formed and Giovanni plunges his arms into the milk, rolling the curd on the bottom of the cauldron and then, like a magician, he pulls out two balls of cheese. These he puts in plastic baskets on a drain board. The rounds of pecorino are aged for thirty days to nine months and will weigh about 3 kilograms each.

The whey is put back on the fire and it is on to making ricotta. It is just after 8:00 am and my eyes are streaming because of the smoke that fills the room. Giovanni collects fig branches and nicks them to get the milky sap running, a natural rennet that works well in fatty sheep's and goat's milk. He throws the branches directly into the whey as it heats, and although a thermometer is consulted, the sound that the wooden stirring stick makes on the bottom of the cauldron is key to knowing when things are ready. Giovanni spoons ricotta into nine plastic baskets (each about 500g). He hands me a spoonful of this totally fresh and warm ricotta, which is sweet and light. The baskets drain into a wooden tray that has a hole on one end, which drains into a bucket that will be mixed with old bread and become part of the pigs' breakfast.

After saying hello to Elisa, who has arrived from town with Sunday lunch, the next chore is to get set up for sheep shearing. Historically, wool was incredibly important to the economy of southern Italy, but in the late 1800s Australian wool offered stiff competition, and then introduction of synthetic fibers in the 20th century led to a collapse in the wool trade. Giovanni doesn't sell the wool because it isn't worth much anymore, but the animals are still sheared once a year to keep them cooler in the hot summer.

The sheep are hard to get into the shearing pen, but all it takes is one to follow Alessio and a juvenile (both making bleating noises) and then they all run in. With about twenty animals jostling for position in the small shed, I can see we have hours of shearing ahead of us.

The animal is rolled onto its back, and with Alessio holding the hind legs, Giovanni shears the belly, then the head, and the hind legs. The sheep is quite calm and just lies there as the clippers ease off the fleece in several large pieces. The animal is slowly rolled over and the shears move along the back and tail. The electric shears mean that depending on how matted the wool is (and the knots hug the skin, making it hard

With no market, the wool is burned because it is worth so little.

to shear without nicking the animal) a single animal can take between five to fifteen minutes to shear. It may help to keep the sheep cool, but shearing is hot work. Sweat drips down Giovanni's face as he moves the shears carefully over the sheep's body. Elisa, Giovanni's wife, comes to help and at some points all three of them have their hands on the animal. How long would this process take before electric shears I wonder?

Once the animal is sheared the wool is put in a bag, the shears are cleaned and blown out with an air compressor, and then it is on to the next sheep. Over the whine of the shears, the sheep inside the shed call to the ones outside, who answer. Swallows play in the yard, flies abound. The sun climbs higher in the sky.

By 12:15 pm there are eleven freshly shorn sheep and three bags of dirty wool to show for over two hours of effort. Although there are more to shear, it will have to wait for another day since the animals are hungry and need to be taken out for a quick bite before our lunch. The animals flow out of the compound and up a small road to the wide open pastures. They are hungry, and there is a twinge of anxiety as they rush to eat whatever is in their path. Although they produce more milk many people don't shepherd goats because they are a lot more work, and as I watch them climbing and eating the olive and cherry trees at the edge of the pasture I can understand why. Like small children with behaviour issues, they need the most attention and management from Giovanni and Alessio. The smell of wild thyme is incredible as the animals crush it underfoot, and a calm descends.

At 2:00 pm we bring the animals back so that we can eat lunch. It's Sunday, and Alessio, three of Giovanni and Elisa's daughters, and one of their boyfriends have come out to the farm. The table is laden with food: pasta with *sugo*, roast chicken (that yesterday was running around in the compound), salad, and fruit. Just after 3:00 pm there is time for cake and gelato for dessert and a coffee before taking the animals back up to the pasture for the rest of the afternoon. The animals are calmer the second time out, and graze their way across the side of a low hill. It is rocky, and there are several caves in the soft limestone. We stand and watch them at the site of an ancient necropolis that was partially excavated in the 1960s, being careful not to fall into the rectangular tombs that were cut out of the bedrock. As we watch the animals graze a distance away from us, I get a better sense of how the dogs work. There are at least twelve dogs that live with Giovanni in the compound, including some puppies. He uses two types of dogs, the large white *Maremmano*, bred to be the guardians of the flock, and the black Italian Shepherd, a breed that is fast, agile, intelligent, and does the work of herding. The *Maremmano* dogs are pretty laid back, and have lived with the sheep since they were puppies so are fiercely loyal. Diana, the Italian Shepherd, stays near Giovanni, appearing to sleep but ever ready to respond to a command. Her

Maremmano dogs are put with the sheep and goats that they protect from the time they are puppies.

89

interactions with the flock to keep them in line, and the darting and sprinting and nipping, looks like mimed hunting; she even looks a bit wolf-like with her gracile build and long pointed snout. A juvenile Italian Shepherd sits with us too, watching and learning. One day he will be in charge of this flock.

Clouds roll across the sky and it threatens to rain, and wind ruffles the long grasses and the goats' hair. Falcons hunt in the fields around us hoping for snakes or butterflies. We stay out in the pastures until just before 7:00 pm, then bring the animals back for the second milking of the day. Baby goats are reunited with their mothers for a feed before the

Giovanni's animals settle into the rolling pasture of the Murgia.

animals are moved into the cave and the milking routine begins. By 7:45 pm the milking is done, with another big plastic bucket to be transformed into cheese in a few days. The shepherd's day is done. For days afterwards my brain wanders back to Giovanni's farm, and with a glance at my watch I can guess what he is doing. When a thunderstorm comes through with torrential rain one afternoon not long after my visit I wonder whether he seeks shelter in a cave, or gets wet along with the flock.

Giovanni clearly represents the hard work and dedication that are essential to being a shepherd. He has not had a day off in over thirty years, but financially he is not well compensated for these efforts. Just as the shepherds of Christ's time were struggling with marginalization, factors beyond a modern shepherd's control threaten this profession with extinction. Italy's entry into the European Union in 1999 has been hard on small food producers. The switch from the lira to the euro meant that Giovanni's milk was worth less. More damaging though, are the sweeping EU regulations meant to address food safety that are blunt instruments and not realistic (or all that necessary) for small producers. Only bigger operations can afford the upgrades in facilities to meet the production regulations, leaving Giovanni and many other shepherds like him with few options. His animals are all tagged and are frequently inspected to offer him the certification required to sell his milk. But milk prices are ridiculously low, about 70 cents for a litre of sheep's milk, meaning that many shepherds work hard for next to nothing. It's no wonder that Italian youth don't want to become shepherds; a growing number of shepherds are immigrants from Eastern Europe or India, who are paid meager wages and believe any work is better than no work. This can make them vulnerable to exploitation while keeping the price of milk low.

Mario and his sheepdog Natasha are from Romania. An immigrant shepherd works someone else's sheep but works with his own dog since communication between shepherd and sheepdog is critical.

If Giovanni had the second form of certification, he could sell his cheese in shops in town. And pecorino sells for over $20 (CDN) per kilogram. But he could not make his cheese in a sooty, smoky room with dogs and cats and turkeys wandering in and out. Hygiene rules dictate stainless steel, standardized sizes of drains in sinks, bathroom facilities, and compromise. Pecorino is often called a *canestrato* cheese, because of the traditional wicker baskets used to form the round shape. These baskets have been deemed unhygienic, so cheese is now made in plastic baskets. Like many other shepherds, Giovanni makes the cheese for personal consumption, which everyone knows means he sells it from his farm or house in town. He sells it for much less than he could get in a store, and always with the worry that inspectors will come and shut things down.

Another thing that people disconnected from their food may not consider is that a shepherd works every day, but only makes cheese for six months of the year, from March through summer. When you can buy milk from the grocery store every day it seems that animals produce milk year round, but milk is generally a seasonal product since animals only produce milk to feed their young, who are born in the spring. Cheese and butter are ingenious ways to preserve milk through the winter, but when you depend on selling it for an income in a modern economy, being idle for half the year is hard. And for the shepherd, he still works in the pastures 365 days a year even if he isn't making cheese. The animals have to eat, so the months when the animals are not producing milk are investments in the flock and the future. These sacrifices, and the ongoing challenges of trying to make a living in an economy that can feel like swimming against the current, do not make shepherding a very attractive profession to Italy's youth. Many question how this form of subsistence can fit in a modern world, and many others are worried that shepherds will fade from the landscape of the Murgia Plateau within a generation.

The challenge is considerable, which becomes obvious when you crunch the numbers of a shepherd's earnings, or drive through parts of Puglia that now look like the monocrops of the Canadian Prairies. After World War II, Italy experienced the "Economic Miracle." Industrialism and modernity were enthusiastically embraced. Tonio remembers as a child in the 1970s that shepherds managed the challenge of feeding their sheep in the summer when the hills were crisp and dry by negotiating access to farmers' fields after they had been harvested. Shepherds would bring their sheep down to graze on the stubbled fields and pay landowners for this grazing access in cheese and manure (which the animals spread where it was needed as they grazed across the fields). But as agriculture industrialized, everything sped up. Today, fields are tilled before shepherds have a chance to graze them. Animals also used to be grazed across fallowed fields, clearing the field ahead of planting and leaving manure as fertilizer for the next crop. Now fields aren't necessarily left fallow since this is considered inefficient, and the development of tractors and chemical fertilizers means there is not the same perceived need for what a shepherd's flock has to offer. Animals are generally kept on their own farms rather than shepherds negotiating use rights, so access is not regulated. Shepherds with no land of their own no longer pay for grazing access in privately-owned landscapes like Fornello (because they cannot afford it) and this makes the shepherds vulnerable. What happens if they are no longer provided access to grazing lands?

Modern technology is also helping to force the hand in favour of farmers through landscape modification. Machines grind up the rocky limestone knolls to transform them into farmable land, although drainage and fertility issues remain, leading to a reliance on additional modern technology. In many places (particularly where irrigation can help to intensify production) the landscape is becoming a singular, mono-cropped one of scale and efficiency, and the once vast pastoral network is shrinking. Carefully protected grazing paths have been usurped by farmers, built over by roads, and encroached by woodlands. Despite having been protected by Italian laws since 1976, statistics from 1998 indicate that of the 3,000 km in southern Italy that were once used as *tratturi*, only 174 km (13%) are in good condition, 113 km (8%) are in a relatively poor condition, 293 km (22%) are in a precarious condition, and 765 km (51%) are no longer visible. These numbers are about twenty years old, so one may imagine an even bleaker picture today.

Another consequence of the industrial food system in southern Italy is that local food producers are not "needed" in the same way; food is much more easily accessible from grocery stores and global food producers/processors than ever before. Synthetic fabrics have been the final nail in the coffin for the wool industry, but cheap food from the farmers of the world--tomatoes and lemons are discussed in this book but there are many examples--makes it very hard for small producers to compete. The intangible cultural values of these producers are subtle, and easily deprioritized. Much is lost when the shepherd disappears from the landscape. Shepherding traditions are woven into the cultural fabric of southern Italy, but the industrial food system, which makes cheap food from global producers alluring and easily accessible, changes the perceived value of shepherds in these communities. It can be overlooked that the soul of cultural identity resides in small local producers like shepherds, whose intimate connections with landscape and inherited cultural knowledge can be undervalued in a drive towards "being modern." But there is more at stake than this. Without shepherds and sheep, land use shifts to a narrow variety of crops; the loss of biodiversity is significant. Walk across a shepherd's pasture and you will notice an incredible variety of wild grasses and herbs, some beautifully fragrant as you walk upon them. Not only does this contribute to the *terroir* of cheese, the tastes of the land reflected in the flavours of real food, it is critical for bees that pollinate the farmers' fields. This ecosystem is used by migratory birds like the magnificent prairie falcon that stops in Matera (as in Altamura and Gravina) to nest and have their young. That the system is integrated is inescapable.

Conservationists are slowly recognizing that traditional farming and shepherding systems like the ones of the Murgia Plateau, which have developed in response to the environmental constraints of the region, have actually been quite beneficial to the ecosystems that occupy these spaces alongside humans. Historically, conservation has focused on "wilderness" without thinking about or valuing the role that humans have had in shaping and maintaining these foodways that are sustainable methods of using marginal landscapes. Low intensity systems don't square well with a modern value system that is measured by scale and efficiency. They are characterized by high human labour input and low yield per hectare, often because they use traditional crop varieties well suited to the harsh environmental conditions at the expense of yield. The *Altamurana* sheep is a great example. For farmers in a dry landscape, key crops have been those that are not overly thirsty because irrigation has not been possible.

Low intensity systems appear to be inefficient when the measure of success is quantity and price. When producers elsewhere can irrigate their crops and produce significantly more per acre (like almonds in California), or produce more lemons without the overhead cost of stone terraces like on the Amalfi Coast, or grow their animals in concentrated feedlots (CAFOs), then these traditional farming systems really seem to be leftovers of the past, no longer meeting the needs of the present. A closer look, though, reveals that there is more than just good cheese at stake here.

Shepherds have a long-standing tradition of sustainably using large areas of grasslands and woodlands. They are connected to their landscape, and when they can manage their flocks and move them across a broad territory to avoid overgrazing, they offer an excellent solution to meeting the challenges of this rocky, dry environment. In contrast, modernity has encouraged intensification, defined as mechanization, irrigation, mono-cropping and a focus on only high-producing varieties. This intensification seems to be a symptom of the disconnect between humans and their landscape. How else to explain the unsustainable use of water, the overuse of chemical fertilizers that then contaminate waters, or the widespread landscape modification like the technology that can grind away the rocky limestone pasture areas of the Murgia Plateau to create marginal land for wheat fields? Since maintaining these low intensity producers is critical, policies must be developed so that they are supported economically and socially to continue to practice them rather than policies like the EU hygiene regulations that seem to have the opposite effect. The measures of success here will be maintaining the amount of land managed in these ways, the maintenance of key food traditions and elements of local identity, and a flush of young shepherds ready to take these traditions forward into the future.

Dignifying shepherding: sheep, shepherds, and tourism

Not so long ago pastoralism was economically relevant for dairy and wool. Rediscovering economic value today may include both the products and the landscapes of shepherds. The *tratturi* are being eyed as a tourist draw similar to the Camino de Santiago pilgrim's walk in Spain, which could be important economically for the region but also in the maintenance of what is left of the pastoral infrastructure. This initiative will get a big boost if the *tratturi* are recognized and protected by UNESCO, a proposal that is currently being reviewed. While reviving the shepherds' tracks is being actively promoted and pursued by local organizations, one cannot help but wonder whether they are remnants of subsistence traditions that are out of sync with a modern world, destined to become memories and components of tourist enterprise. The goal in parts of southern Italy where shepherding is still practiced can be more than the economic benefit of tourism. If integrated foodways are to be maintained or reinvigorated, *tratturi* are critical; shepherds *must* move their flocks to access grazing areas, otherwise the subsistence pattern falls apart. Creating pathways that allow tourists to appreciate the pastoralist experience and "walk a mile in their shoes" is of limited cultural value if pastoralism is not promoted in these contemporary landscapes. Tourist encounters with shepherds and their flocks using these tracks as they have done for centuries creates the ultimate agritourism opportunity to walk alongside and gain a deeper, more authentic appreciation for the many contributions that pastoralists have made to food, culture and landscape.

Beyond maintaining shepherding landscapes, a concerted effort is needed to maintain the shepherds themselves, and the knowledge embedded in a tradition now largely sustained by elder shepherds and immigrants. While many local food producers lament the fact that young Italians don't seem to want to work hard as food producers (and are not necessarily very welcoming of foreign workers), it is interesting to note that in 2012 the agricultural union Coldiretti reported that the profession had recently attracted 3,000 young Italians. The timing coincides with the national unemployment rate topping 10% (and a youth unemployment rate of over 30%). Coldiretti said the unexpected influx of shepherds under the age of 35 was helping to rejuvenate a sector of Italian agriculture that had become the preserve of older farmers, many of whom would take their wealth of knowledge with them to the grave. According to the report, in nearly 80% of cases, young shepherds have introduced more advanced animal husbandry techniques and improved the quality of the meat, wool, and cheese they produce. This may be a tangible result of the Slow Food movement, and part of a broader reconnection with food production that is seeing youth enter these professions as dignified artisans. It must be celebrated and supported, and to do this there must be both a sustainable landscape to produce their products and a sustainable market to sell their products so that they may be economically successful while promoting and protecting important cultural food traditions.

There are some creative initiatives that are breaking the mould in terms of economic and social development. Slow Food actively engages with local groups to promote "artisan" products through their "Ark of Taste" and finds new markets for small producers. In Abruzzo consumers can connect with producers through an "adopt a sheep" project, where customers fund the shepherd and get cheese products sent to them in return. While this will appeal to many who value rural products and lifestyles, Tonio has a more direct connection in mind. Messors' Fornello Project (described in chapter 3) aims to generate benefits for local shepherds and tourists in a participatory type of agritourism. The objective is to celebrate quality food by reconnecting disenchanted urban dwellers with the landscape and people who make food. The cheese- making workshops that take place in the reclaimed shepherd's house serve as knowledge and cultural exchanges with benefits for both visitors and shepherds. Fresh cheeses are eaten on the spot for lunch, and shared with a passing shepherd; the pecorino cheese to be aged in the caves on site represents the hope of the future.

Modernity has crippled local foodways, but may offer creative forms of reinvigoration as well. Globalization has immigrant shepherds in Italian landscapes because the pay is so minimal and shepherding has been devalued as a profession. Modern EU regulations make it difficult to compete. Yet the tools of globalization such as the Internet will be part of advertising the workshops so that participants from around the world can come and connect with food in new ways, as well as connect with a global consumer market to sell the cheese for a price that reflects the care and craft involved. Shepherding must be recast in this modern frame rather than expecting a romantic timelessness. This flexibility and dynamism of culture is represented by the rebirth of the stone shepherd's house at Fornello, an old building that is being restored in a new world. Changing the old to work in a new setting is very different from North American preservation ethics that value the "pristine," which seems to freeze things in time; this turns them into passive museum pieces rather than things, places, or ideas that continue to be relevant even as contexts change. Reinvigorating the cultural, social and economic functions of the site breathes new life into this landscape that has been repeatedly transformed over the centuries. And so I stand in the cool of the building, looking out the door into the bright sunlight, and watch the sheep grazing in front of me. The grasses and herbs they eat now become the milk for tomorrow's cheese, a magical gift celebrating the connections to this place

10. Tasting the Landscape, Tasting the Past: A crash course in *terroir* and other sources of diversity

On a warm day in late May of 2016 I joined Giovanni Maino and his flock of sheep and goats on a walk through the pastures behind his small farm compound. When the animals first go out in the morning they are hungry and move quickly over the landscape, but after they have been able to satisfy their hunger pangs they settle down and graze more leisurely. What they eat gives their milk a unique flavour, which in turn gives Giovanni's cheese its intense, robust tones. And unlike the cheese from a large industrial facility purchased at a grocery store that you can be fairly confident will taste the same every time you buy it, every small run of pecorino and ricotta will produce a slightly different cheese. This moving target of flavour is called *terroir*, which is considered the character of a food shaped by the many changing elements of the environment, an expression of the food's connection to the landscape in time and space. Sometimes *terroir* is described as "the taste of place," literally capturing a snapshot of the landscape and variation in weather that leave their mark in the resulting food products.

Terroir is much easier to understand once you have walked across the pastures of the Murgia Plateau. This arid, Mediterranean, steppe environment has been shaped both naturally (through the erosion of the karst limestone) and culturally (the grazing of sheep and goats, and light seasonal burns) for thousands of years. At first glance these grasslands appear quite bleak, but look closer and you notice that they are covered in an incredible variety of small herbs and grasses. In May white chamomile flowers dot the fields and aromatic wild thyme and mint waft through the air as you walk across the pastures and crush the plants underfoot.

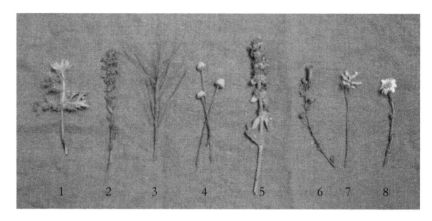

1. Tumble thistle(*Gundelia touine fortii*)
2. Basil thyme (*Acinos arvensis*)
3. Eastern tumble mustard (*Sisymbrium orientale*)
4. Mayweed chamomile (*Anthemis cotula*)
5. Mint family (not further identified)
6. Bellflower (*Campanula sps.*)
7. Parsnip (*Berula erecta*)
8. Chamomile (*Chamaemelum nobile*)
9. Wild buckwheat (*Polygonum sp.*)
10. Cudweed (*Gnaphalium sylvaticum*)
11. Wild oregano (*Origanum vulgare*)
12. Owl clover (*Orthacarpus sp.*)
13. Mint family (not further identified)
14. Hare's tail grass (*Lagurus ovatus*)
15. Common oat (*Avena sativa*)
16. Durum wheat (*Triticum durum*)
* A short euphorbia was also present but not collected.

In late May, the pastures of the Murgia Plateau offer a varied menu.

Sheep are quite picky eaters, sticking mainly to the grasses. Goats, however, are not, and will mow down anything in their path. This can include prickly, thistle-like plants and euphorbia (which are generally toxic to other animals). I watched goats practically climb into a cherry tree to steal the last remaining fruit and prune blooming olive trees as they were moved quickly past them. Giovanni told me that a few years ago goats cleared the fields of the giant fennel plants (*Ferula communis*) in a number of days. It should come as no surprise that what is eaten will be tasted in the animals' milk, and these flavours change from sheep to goat and over the course of the season as various plants appear, flower, then wither.

The composition of milk also changes over the season. Spring milk is generally fattier and sweeter because it contains more colostrum and is specifically designed for the needs of newborn lambs and kids. The quantity of milk also changes, and so too the proportion of goat to sheep milk in the resulting cheese. These variations highlight the seasonality of the product.

Terroir for wine (the original context for this term) is a combination of soils, climate, and weather. (The difference between weather and climate is a measure of time. Weather describes conditions of the atmosphere over a short period of time, while climate is the average of weather over a longer period of time.) Poor, exposed soils that are often not good for other crops are redeemed when they grow forgiving grapevines. In Puglia, the Primitivo grape offers a striking example of *terroir*. Grown on the Murgia Plateau, these grapes have more acidity due to the limestone soils, but further to the south, in the heel of Italy's boot, it is warmer and the Adriatic and Ionian seas influence the *terroir* of the same grapes. Not only does the proximity to the ocean impart a slight saltiness to the air, but the ocean winds also mitigate the heat. Depending on *terroir*, Primitivo wines can have a pleasant fruitiness, with hints of sour or black cherry, or a spiciness containing pepper and liquorice as well as hints of Mediterranean vegetation.

Sommeliers explain that when people talk about a wine's vintage (a concept unique to wine in tandem with *terroir*), they are really talking about weather. The amount and timing of rain, heat spikes, frosts, and snow all have consequences, from the beginning of the growth season through to the time that the grape is picked. Ripe grapes, for example, that experience a rainstorm just before they are picked, will absorb water and dilute the resulting wine (one of the reasons why grapes generally aren't picked right after a heavy rain).

A wine's vintage is a celebration of diversity and the specific conditions of a particular year. It tells the story of the year it was produced, and in this way it is bottled history. This history gives wine a heart and a soul. This is particularly poignant when there is a connection to the producers; many vineyards have been passed down through generations of family, and so an aged bottle of wine represents family history too, a time capsule that links generations and is a reminder of a specific time and place. The people who made the wine may be gone by the time it is consumed, making old bottles of wine very nostalgic.

For a wine maker, it can be almost like stepping back in time, into the vineyard, and recalling the sunshine or rain of a particular year. One experience stands out for me in my dawning awareness of what *terroir* means. In 2015 I shared a bottle of Tonio's homemade wine that had been bottled in 2002. That the bottle still existed had come as a surprise (it had been thoughtfully saved by our friend Francesco to be shared when the time was right), and Tonio was excited to see how it had aged. I had never consumed wine alongside the person who had picked the grapes and then made the wine, and Tonio's personal connection provided an intimate sense of how *terroir* influences the food but also shapes the people who produce it. As he sipped the wine, its brownish red hues swirling in the glass, Tonio remembered planting the vines amongst the olive trees on the family farm when he was a child. He remembered the few years that he bottled the wine rather than storing it in giant vats, and remembered drinking the wine at his wedding. Finally, he remembered ripping the vines out in 2010 after thirty-five years because they were increasingly shaded by the olive trees. As Tonio drank the wine he said he could taste these memories, his vineyard, and the fava beans that grew nearby, the ultimate expression of context and connections made through food.

Wine and cheese have personalities; they are living and dynamic, and evolve through their lifetimes. Both products are manipulated by humans to control decay. As a living entity housing a wealth of microbes, the flavour of milk is changing from the moment it splashes into the milking bucket, oxidizes, and ages. Microbes are responsible for the transformation of cheese as it ages; these microbes are in the milk, which are joined by additional microbes in the caves where the wheels are aged, the microclimates of which encourage a parade of different species of microbe to populate and work their magic on the developing cheese.

Wine wants to become vinegar eventually, so aging it properly in terms of temperature and humidity is important, and clearly contributes to its flavour. As in cheese caves, microbes in cellars play active roles in this dynamic process. Because of alcohol in the air, which evaporates from wooden casks or slowly slips past a cork, a black cellar mold (*Racodium cellare*) is a discerning inhabitant of Europe's best old cellars. The mold, which as Charles Badham so evocatively described in 1863, *"festoons [a cellar's] ceiling, shags its walls and wraps its thick coat round wine-casks,"* nurtures the air to stave off the mustiness of dank, dark places. The fresh air, in turn, contributes to the developing flavours of the aging wines.

Appreciating *terroir* is in direct contrast to the homogenization of the industrial food system. But it is interesting to break down the erosion of *terroir* to understand how it changes in a modern world. Modern techniques and hygiene requirements are changing the flavours of wine and cheese in many ways. While the flavour and composition of Giovanni's milk changes throughout the year based on what his animals eat, in industrial-scale dairy production, the animals' diet is carefully crafted to maximize milk yield. Rather than the variation that comes from natural pastures, the industrial diet consists of forage (basically replicating natural pasture grasses with a focus on barley, alfalfa, and increasingly corn) and a blended product called "concentrate," which is a combination of proteins, carbohydrates, minerals, fats, and vitamins from items like distillers grains, corn, oats, wheat, molasses, beet pulp, canola meal, and vegetable oil. Eating a consistent diet means more continuity in the taste of industrially produced dairy.

Historically, raw milk was used to make cheese. The development of pasteurization and the dawning of the Hygiene Movement in the late 1800s has changed this, with many policies now requiring that milk be pasteurized before use. For Stilton cheese to be called Stilton cheese, for example, in keeping with the coveted PDO (Protected Designation of Origin) production protocol, drawn up in 1996 by the Stilton Cheese Makers Association, only pasteurized milk can be used. This creates an interesting situation: PDO status is meant to protect the authenticity of a product, and Stilton has been made in central England for hundreds of years. There is now only one small producer that makes this cheese with raw milk, arguably maintaining the integrity of authenticity, but he is not allowed to call his cheese "Stilton" (he calls it Stichelton instead, the original name for the town of Stilton). The argument is that pasteurization makes milk safer from pathogenic microbes that can make consumers sick. Pasteurization is a heat treatment that kills harmful microbes, but acts as a blunt instrument; the process cannot target just the pathogens. The result is that pasteurized milk is no longer living; its microbes that contribute to the magical transformation of cheese are utterly compromised. What is interesting about microbes in aged cheeses though, is that the good ones generally fend off the nasty ones like E. coli, listeria, and salmonella. In the right conditions (like small-scale operations), pasteurization is not necessary for aged cheeses. Microbes work on the cheese in waves; one species creates an environment to support the next in a succession of species, out-competing the pathogens. Although most European PDO cheeses continue to use raw milk (only 8% of European cheeses with PDO status currently require the use of pasteurized milk), Slow Food International cautions that 53% of cheeses lack specific indications regarding the heat treatment of milk. This ambiguity could easily lead to the increased use of pasteurized milk and the homogenization of unique cheeses.

Microbes are introduced throughout the process of making cheese. A trend in industrial cheese production is the use of pre-selected cultures, which consist of a limited number of microbes. Traditional cheeses are inoculated with the residual microbes from previous batches, which leads to incredible microbial wealth. This is one reason why traditional cheeses can have much more complex flavours than modern, controlled-inoculation cheeses. Microbes are also present in production facilities and work surfaces; recent hygiene regulations have required facilities to upgrade to stainless steel vats and plastic molding baskets because they are easier to clean and microbe-free. However, experiments conducted by Noella Marcellino, a Benedictine nun and cheese making with a PhD in microbiology, successfully showed that while bad microbes thrived in the stainless steel vat required to meet FDA regulations, these same microbes died off in the wooden barrel; they were no match for the other, beneficial microbes that outcompeted them. Shepherds on the Murgia Plateau no longer use the wicker *canestrato* baskets for forming pecorino cheese, and while the plastic replacements are easier to buy and more hygienic, they do not harbour the microbes that would have set to work immediately in the wicker molds to age the cheese. Remember, aging cheese is controlled decay.

The wine industry is experiencing similar changes: the shift from wood barrels to stainless steel is wiping out the benevolent molds that once were the sign of a good cellar. Steel barrels prevent alcohol from evaporating into the air, and without this necessary part of the cellar ecosystem, molds are starved. (Without the benign molds, it is possible for other, less friendly molds to invade these dark places, requiring the use of antifungal agents.)

Thinking about the many factors that contribute to the tastes of food reaffirms the many connections between humans, plants, animals, the landscape, weather and the seasons…in short, the universe. Losing the flavours of place and history in food, and the stories of producers, is a pricy tradeoff in the realm of industrialized food that is stripped of humanity and provenance. To borrow the French appreciation of diversity: "*Vive la différence!*"

11. Cheese

Dessert without cheese is like a beauty with only one eye.
-Jean Anthelme Brillat-Savarin

Nowhere is the concept of living cultures more apt than when considering the process of cheese making. A host of invisible micro-organisms parade through different acts in a complex play that, depending on the desired cheese, may be hours long, or months. While the wisdom of the shepherd is important to cheese making, it is these microbes that are ultimately in control of the process. By managing conditions in the production and aging of cheese, be it temperature, humidity, or the timing and use of salt, the cheese maker is the maestro, the microbes the orchestra, and the cheese the art. Most of the cheeses in Puglia are peasant cheeses, fairly simple to make and store, not aged for very long periods of time, and not overly strong like Gorgonzola. As with pickling vegetables or curing meat, making cheese is a way to store milk, extending its shelf life and making the most of every product the landscape offers. Industrialized eaters may be forgiven for forgetting that milk is a seasonal product, timed to and based on the rhythms of calving and lambing from the spring through summer. This seasonal product perishes very quickly in the heat of southern Italy, and prior to the invention of refrigeration, cheese-making technology was a crucial innovation to store the nutrients of dairy for consumption in the lean months of winter. As Sister Noella, the Benedictine "cheese nun" from Connecticut puts it, cheese producers are tasked with controlling decay, and cheese is "delicious rot."

There is a magic to cheese, how the same basic ingredient can be transformed into a variety of beautiful soft and hard cheeses, some of which are meant to be eaten fresh and others that need to be aged. Through working with different shepherds and cheese mongers I have come to appreciate these complexities, the intricate knowledge behind the transformations that represents generations of wisdom about how the process works. It is very satisfying to participate directly with cheese producers to connect with this food, from pasture to plate.

Cheese starts with coagulation, which generally requires something to curdle the milk. Traditionally, rennet is extracted from the stomach of a calf or lamb since this is the enzyme that helps with the digestion of milk proteins. The natural enzyme present in the first two months of a calf's life allows the animal's body to digest milk while it is breastfeeding. (Human babies have this enzyme too, which is what makes regurgitated milk burps look curdled.)

There are other sources of rennet like the acid from lemons and thistles (*Cardoun*); in Puglia a traditional shepherd technique is to use fig twigs since they have a milky sap in them that curdles the whey. I have witnessed various methods of using the fig branches: some shepherds score the branches and throw them directly into the milk when it reaches 85 degrees Celsius, while others cut the branches into short sections and put them in water, which is then strained and added to the warming milk. Fig twigs generally work best with sheep's milk because it is fattier; when using fig branches with cow's milk the fig twigs are supplemented with citric acid.

Lamb stomachs are harvested and dried for the rennet. Fig branches are easily collected locally in Puglia as a source of vegetable rennet.

The process begins with milk heated in a giant cauldron to between 37-40 degrees Celsius. The rennet is added and given time to work. Coagulation time depends on the degree of acidity, the grade of fat, and the kind of milk (sheep, goat, or cow). Sheep's milk is fattier so coagulates faster, while cow's milk takes 15-20 minutes. Once coagulated, the curd is stirred and broken up. There are two components that are worked separately to make different products: curds, which sink to the bottom become cheese, and the watery whey, which becomes ricotta.

Curds

There are many cheeses that are made in Puglia from the curd of cows, sheep and goats. Cows' milk is used for fresh cheeses like *mozzarella*, *burrata*, and *primosale*, as well as *scamorza* and *caciocavallo*. Sheep and goats milk curds are sometimes made into fresh cheeses, but generally in this region they are aged and transformed into rounds of salty and sharp-tasting *pecorino*.

Blocks of curd await their transformation into stretch cheeses.

For mozzarella, day-old curds are generally used. The curd is turned out onto a marble slab and cools into a soft, solid block. This slight aging gives the curds time to acidify, allowing them to be stretched in hot water. The blocks are shaved into long slices and put in a large bowl. Very hot water is added and the contents of the bowl are stirred until a magical transformation begins before your very eyes: the pieces of solid curd combine to become a soft mass that can be stretched like taffy until it is shiny and smooth. A long strand of stretch mozzarella is then pulled from the bowl and made into small and large balls, like *bocconcini*, small knots, braids, or even whimsical animals (I have seen a particularly convincing elephant!). The completed forms rest in salted water or whey, and are best eaten fresh.

A delicious cheese native to Puglia is *burrata*. Apparently it is a fairly recent invention; locals claim that farmers dreamed up *burrata* as a way to use up extra cow's milk or water buffalo milk curds. The curds are stretched to form a mozzarella pouch, which then holds small scraps of curd and cream. Another local variation is to put a thin slice of pear inside along with the cream and curd scraps. *Burrata* is usually wrapped in asphodel leaves to remind people to eat it very fresh (within 48 hours); if the leaves have started to turn brown the cheese is too old! When you cut into this cheese, the soft

Fresh balls of bocconcini become part of a tomato and basil salad.

mozzarella exterior yields easily to the knife to reveal a slow ooze of cheesy cream. No wonder it is called *"burrata,"* which is Italian for "buttery."

Other stretch curd cheeses made in Puglia that are aged (and sometimes smoked) rather than enjoyed fresh include *scamorza* and *caciocavallo*. Both can be made with either cow or sheep's milk, although cow's milk is most common. *Caciocavallo* tastes a bit like Provolone (although many proud locals will deny this!). The cheese is salted to create a rind as it air dries. It has a distinctive, squat bowling pin shape that gives the cheese its name; the neck accommodates a string that allows the cheese to be hung to dry and age, but also historically it helped it be transported down from the hill pastures and shepherd's *jazzi* by being slung across a horse's saddle.

Vito, a farmer who has been making cheese for over 25 years on the Murgia Plateau, makes Manteca. Similar to burrata, the mozzarella is quickly stretched around a ball of butter, which melts as it is enveloped by the fresh, warm cheese.

106

The birth of pecorino cheese: Giovanni rolls the curds into balls on the bottom of the cauldron, then pulls them out and presses them into plastic baskets. The baskets on the left make 3kg wheels of pecorino that are aged for anywhere from one to nine months.

After settling for a few minutes the soft curds are carefully flipped out and put back into the basket upside down. The basket leaves distinctive impressions on the surfaces of the cheeses, even ones like primosale (at the left) that are eaten right away. Once the rounds of pecorino have been salted a few times they are left to age (below). Some shepherds rub the surfaces of the cheese with olive oil periodically to manage the molds.

Caciocavallo podolico from Masseria Fiori in Gargano.

Another way to process the curd is to press it into a round mold or basket. On the Murgia Plateau cheeses made with wicker baskets are called *canestrato* cheeses. The whey drains out of the basket as the curd is pressed into it, giving the cheese its form. Because the reed baskets are hard to clean they have been victims of EU hygiene regulations; today plastic baskets are generally used.

The next step is to salt the cheese. Salt stops the acidification of cheese, allowing it to dry and age. Different cheeses are aged for different lengths of time, creating variations in rind and flavour due to the different suites of microbes that participate in the process. *Primosale* means "first salt," indicating a fresh cheese that has been lightly salted only once. In contrast, two to three months of aging produces a rind and mold, and for a hard cheese that can be grated it must be aged longer (at least six months). The aging is done in a cool, dark place; the caves of the Murgia Plateau are perfect.

Whey

Once the curd has been won from the cloudy, watery whey, it is time for the next product: ricotta. Ricotta means "recooked," indicating that the whey needs to be reheated. Sometimes a bit of raw milk is added as the whey reaches its maximum temperature of 85 degrees Celsius, which introduces a bit more fat and gives the ricotta more body and flavour. Salt is also added for taste. At 85 degrees the fig twigs are added; the whey curdles immediately, and the heat is turned off. The solids are skimmed off the top and put in small plastic baskets. Nothing of value is wasted: some shepherds will make whey butter from the last remnants of fat in the whey, but often the liquid feeds the farm's animals.

Fresh baskets of ricotta cool and drain in a wooden tray before being sold to customers at Giovanni's farm.

Fresh ricotta keeps for two to three days in the refrigerator (one of the few things that earns a spot in the small *masseria* fridges besides raw meat and white wine), but after that it can be shaken every day for about three months and housed in a glass or terracotta jar to make *ricotta forte*, a Pugliese specialty. It has a very strong flavour, and the unusual quality of creating a dry sensation on your teeth and gums. The acid of tomatoes might cut this quality in the context of bruschetta; sadly I tried it plain on a piece of bread and had a hard time finishing the mouthful.

12. Wine

Nunc est bibendum. (Now is the time to drink.)
-Horace

Wine--red, white, sparkling, sweet, dry, spicy...In a glass it is almost human, with legs and a nose; a compliment may be that it is full-bodied. Italy is the world's largest wine producer, and viticulture has been honed and encouraged for millennia. For the Romans wine was one of the few things that everyone had access to. The life of a slave would have been harsh, but even he had wine to soften the edges of a hard life, to enjoy as an everyday beverage. Everyone drank wine, perhaps because the water of cities would have been increasingly dirty and disease ridden. With this intense demand, wine seems to have been an important catalyst for the expansion of the Roman Empire, and in turn the diffusion of viticulture to the provinces: Gaul, Spain, France, Germany. The economics of wine was significant. Vessels plied the Mediterranean, connecting the vineyard producers with consumers, and ceramic amphorae were common cargoes for the transportation of wine throughout the Roman world.

In the story of wine, connections between the beverage and sacrifice are made often. A vintner may have a lot to say about this connection. Because grapes can be temperamental in response to the weather, and harvest time is labour intensive, it can be hard to make a profit in wine. In a time before technological help, ancient agronomists estimate that vineyards required three times more labourers than olive groves or wheat farming, and high quality wine demanded even more labour, creating a downward pressure on the quality of wine to maximize the quantity produced. Indeed, the land use tensions--grow grains for bread or grapes for wine--speak to sacrifices and compromise, with multiple factors tipping the balance one way or the other over time.

For millennia wine has been associated with rebirth and life, possibly because the vine appears to die in the winter and then revive with vigorous growth in the spring. In ancient farming communities of the Mediterranean, where the fertility of the fields was paramount, the vine became a symbol of the cyclical rebirth of nature as a whole. Along with bread and olives, grapes came to represent the spoils of agriculture. It is not too surprising that the various gods of wine share an association with agricultural fertility rituals in the religions where viticulture was practiced. Add to this the fact that wine is the same colour as blood and its use as a sacrificial item is all but guaranteed. If one needs further proof of wine's legitimacy as a "divine fluid," all you need consider is the sensation of being intoxicated; the Greeks explained that buzzed feeling of "other-worldliness" as being in the presence of the gods. With a 15 percent alcohol content (compared to perhaps 4 percent for beer, and in a world before fermented spirits), no other beverage could create quite the same type of experience.

The symbolism and religious importance of wine helped spread the grape and associated wine culture from as early as 6,000 BC on the borders of the modern states of Turkey, Syria, and Iraq throughout the Mediterranean. While many have argued that the Greeks brought grapevines with them to the Italian peninsula in the 8th century BC, archaeological evidence now seems quite clear that wine was already being enjoyed by the Etruscans when Greeks arrived in southern Italy to found the city state colonies of *Magna Graecia*. By the 5th century BC, Greeks were referring to the southern Italian peninsula as *Oenotria*, "the land of vines," suggesting that grapes were an ever more popular crop. The Greeks likely influenced the production of wine by introducing new varieties and growing techniques, new opportunities to consume it, particularly in the ritual context of the *symposium* (from the Greek *sympinein* "to drink together"). The symposium was a place for elite men to debate, celebrate athletic victories, and discuss important topics of the day, all accompanied by music and wine. The host would decide how strong the wine for the evening would be, and mix water and wine accordingly (the Greeks, and later Romans considered the drinking of pure wine a habit of the uncivilized). To be fair, typical Greek wines would have been both sweet and high in alcohol content, so adding water would have been important for making them lighter and easier to drink. (The same cannot be said for the popular additions of various flavourings like sea water, spices, honey and resin!)

The ritual artifacts required for symposia, such as the *krater*, a large jar from which the wine was drawn, and drinking bowls, are common tomb inclusions in pre-Roman crypts such as those investigated at Botromagno near Gravina. Another interesting piece of ritual paraphernalia found in high status male tombs in Italy from the 8th and 7th centuries BC is a bronze grater, whose use is described by Homer in the *Iliad*. The grater was used to prepare a beverage called *kukeon* to "promote good conversations," a mixture of wine, grated cheese, honey, and a sprinkle of barley groats. One can just imagine the debate, merrymaking, storytelling, and offering of libations to both gods and ancestors that was facilitated by the consumption of wine! Maybe this is what the great Roman poet Horace was alluding to when he declared, "No poem was ever written by a drinker of water." Clearly, the symposium, and the consumption of wine in this context, was a common frame of reference; with ultimate roots stretching back to the Phoenician traditions of the Levant it illustrates the sharing of goods, culture and ideas across a broad geography. We are reminded, once again, of the many influences that have contributed to southern Italy's complex food traditions.

The symposium (and the Roman equivalent, the *convivium*), was reserved for the rich, but over time the appeal of wine in Italy flowed down the social ladder and was consumed by all. Everyone drank wine, from emperor to slave, and from cradle to grave, and beyond. The Romans believed that the invisible essence of a person (called the Shades or Manes) lingered around their remains after death (along with their ability to enjoy bodily pleasures), creating the opportunity for the living to periodically visit and feast alongside their ancestors. Tombs were often built as venues for these activities, and included libation tubes made out of lead or terracotta that would run from the surface down to or near the mouth of the deceased so that the ancestor could receive wine. Snakes often hid in these tubes and would slither out when wine was poured down them, so snakes were considered the earthly manifestation of the Shades. The Shades were the hosts of these parties, which often stretched late into the evening, and these feasts and wine soaked events were important opportunities to maintain social immortality since all guests would toast the host and appreciate their hospitality. According to Banksy (a UK graffiti artist), you die twice: "one time when you stop breathing and a second time, a bit later on, when somebody says your name for the last time." With wine representing rebirth and an afterlife, its use to connect the living and the dead in tomb side rituals is particularly poignant.

By the 1st century BC wine economics were in flux. Cato the Censor (234-149 BC) writes that annual per capita consumption was about seven amphorae, but slaves doing hard labour were given more, as much as ten amphorae a year. Slaves had access to very low quality wine that was made by mixing water with the pulp left over after the grapes were pressed; even so, with the average amphora capacity of 22 litres of wine, the allocation of wine to slaves in chain gangs would be equivalent to 220 litres, or 293 contemporary 750 mL bottles!

Supply increased in a few ways to meet the demand. Rather than subsistence farmers growing grapes for their own consumption, wine was increasingly produced on large villa estates, representing a significant shift in agrarian economy towards something more like cash cropping. (The sheer number of wine amphorae speaks to the volume of production and distribution.) Much of the labour on these estates would have been done by slaves acquired from the provinces in exchange for wine to quench the considerable thirsts of the likes of the Gauls, whose consumption was amplified by drinking the wine straight instead of diluted. As more and more land was absorbed into the villa estates, the rural populations, finding themselves displaced, migrated to urban centres; by the 1st century BC Rome had one million inhabitants. The demand for wine increased in these urban centres, a cycle that changed both economic and farming landscapes. The eruption of Mt. Vesuvius in AD 79 buried not only the cities of Pompeii and Herculaneum, but also a great swath of vineyards in the area surrounding the volcano. This natural disaster threatened to interrupt the trade of wine because Pompeii's port was destroyed, which affected people far beyond the extent of the ash clouds. This amplified a trend to replant wheat fields with vineyards.

Wine was stored and transported in tapered jars called amphorae with distinctive handles around the narrow neck that was sealed with a cork. Amphorae generally held about 22 litres (nearly 7 gallons) of wine. Predictably, these containers were extremely heavy when full, which favoured transportation by boat instead of overland. This affected the geographic distribution and economics of wine quite significantly: it was cheaper to move wine by boat the length of the Mediterranean than to transport it more than one hundred kilometers by land. Consequently, vineyards tended to be located near the coast or river corridors.

More and more wine was imported from the provinces to meet demand, and coupled with domestic factors, it was inevitable that eventually the Italian peninsula would be awash in wine. Like the quality of the wine, the prices slumped, the uncertainty and challenges of the vintner confirmed. This is likely the economic reason behind the Domitian edict of AD 92, whereby no new vineyards could be created and half of the existing vineyards in the provinces were ripped out and replaced with wheat. This edict, which lasted two hundred years, had profound consequences on the development of wine culture in Western Europe. It not only protected the domestic wine industry from competition but preserved the supply of grain: humans cannot survive

A fresco on a wall of a take away restaurant (the tops of the ceramic serving pots visible in the countertop) shows Bacchus (second from the left) holding a drinking horn in one hand, while the ancestors (Shades) assemble below in the form of snakes.

on wine alone, even the best wine.

Pompeii is a fine place to appreciate Roman wine culture. The preservation and extensive excavations provide a great picture of what sipping wine would have been like 2,000 years ago. At one of the two hundred taverns in the city you could put down your coins and watch as your red wine was drawn from a clay amphora stored under the counter and handed to you in an earthenware mug. You may be surprised by your first sip: Romans enjoyed quite sweet wines, and sometimes heated it or included spices. The sweetness was accomplished in part by picking the grapes late in the fall after the first frost, which concentrates the sugars in the fruit, or (in the case of *mulsum*) adding honey just before drinking.

From wine prices posted on the walls we can see that a pint cost one, two, three, or four *asses* per *sextarius* depending on quality; by comparison, a loaf of bread cost two *asses*. By the time of the eruption it was known that some grape varieties produced wines best consumed young, before they became too bitter (or turned to vinegar); the majority of wines available at tavern prices would have been aged for no more than a year. However, there were others, like the much hyped Falernian, a full-bodied varietal grown on the border of Latium and Campania in the south, that were considered better as they matured. According to Pliny, this white wine was aged for ten to twenty years, until it was the colour of amber. The aging of wine added to the precarious nature of viticulture, making it both an art and a science; as Pliny observed, "Nothing experienced a greater increase in value than wine that had been cellared up to twenty years or a greater decrease in value afterwards."

Some wonder whether the appearance of these taverns, evidence of broad consumption of wine across the social classes, encouraged the boom in new vineyards that sprouted up in the 1st century. Many of these were located within the city walls of Pompeii. Beginning in the 1970s, the University of Maryland excavated one such vineyard and associated villa, and much work in the past several decades has been devoted to researching the ancient viticulture of the area. The *Villa dei Misteri* (Villa of the Mysteries) has lent its name to the experimental archaeology project that was initiated in 1996 between the Archaeological Superintendent of Pompeii and the Mastroberardino winery.

This vineyard, located just north of the amphitheatre, was excavated in 1970 by the University of Maryland, and is now part of the Villa dei Misteri project. We looked through the gate and gazed upon the vines as we drank Pompeiano Rosso, a very good reason to walk through Pompeii carrying a wine glass in your bag.

Many of the vineyards that accompanied the beautiful villas within the walls of Pompeii have been replanted and a small amount of wine is produced each year. Root casts and DNA studies of charred seeds have helped to identify the grape varieties that were being grown in AD 79 (Aglianico, Piedirosso and Sciascinoso), which were replanted using the same holes for the vine spacing and chestnut stakes , and the same pruning and vine training techniques. (Both excavations and texts from Pliny the Elder suggest a system of stakes with crossbars.) The project has adopted many Roman winemaking techniques, such as not filtering the wine prior to bottling, to provide the taste experience of wine from ancient Pompeii from start to finish.

One can truly appreciate the importance of context when you sip a glass of 2002 Pompeiano Rosso (a blend of 90% Piedirosso and 10% Sciascinoso) next to the recently-restored, frescoed room in the Villa dei Misteri, having just walked past these re-established vineyards. The frescos depict the initiation rites into Bacchic "mysteries," a reinvention of the Bacchus cult that was banned by the Roman senate for its "morally corrupt" drunken revelry, dancing, and sex. Bacchus was the Roman name for the Greek god Dionysus, god of wine, who was also associated with the afterlife and the cycles of death and rebirth. Because only 25,000 kilograms of grapes are produced in the town per year (just over 1200 bottles of wine per vintage), a bottle has to be ordered six months in advance--and at 130 euros per bottle it is not likely a wine I will drink very often. It may not have been the best wine I drank in Italy, but in context, having just walked through the streets of Pompeii, with one of the vineyards in a walled garden just behind us, it made for one of the most memorable glasses of wine I have ever had.

Italian wine culture today

During the Roman period, Italian wine was in its prime. However, quality slowly slipped as farmers prioritized quantity over quality to meet the demand for cheap wine by the new lower class, consumer market. After the fall of Rome the demand for wine dwindled. Wine knowledge was maintained by monks, who continued to produce wine through the medieval period and in so doing preserved the techniques that were then available when wine gained popularity again in the Renaissance.

On the Italian peninsula wine remained part of the informal economy, a product made on farms and traded as partial compensation for labour at harvest time. In the early 20th century, Italian wine was criticized for its poor quality in a rapidly globalizing market (think large chianti bottles wrapped in burlap twine!), and the government introduced regulations designed to improve quality. These regulations must have worked; today Italian wines are considered by critics to be amongst the best in the world.

Italy is the largest wine-producing country in the world and Puglia generally contributes from 18 to 20 percent of the country's total, more than any other region. Until recently, Puglia produced bulk wine, and its wine was generally considered "rustic" and "rough," which doesn't sound very complimentary. This wine was either consumed locally or shipped north for the supermarket export trade. In the last ten to fifteen years though the *terroir* of Puglia has been "discovered," and the robust, varied flavours that come from the limestone soils and fairly dry climate has fueled a "Wine Rush." New wineries have sprung up and old ones have seen the infusion of capital; prepare to see more Pugliese wine in North American liquor stores!

There are three main varieties of warm weather grapes that are grown in Puglia for red wine. Negroamaro is almost exclusively grown in Puglia and is the most widely planted variety. When it arrived in Puglia is unclear, but it is considered one of Italy's most ancient wines. It seems likely that it arrived with the Greek colonists in the 8th century BC; the rocky, arid landscape really agreed with this varietal, and it is often referred to as native to the Salento region. Since the name likely comes from a fusion of the Greek word *mavros* and the Latin word *niger* (both meaning black, in reference to the colour of the grapes), this wine is literally called "black black."

The most famous grape of the province is Primitivo, a sweet yet dry wine with berry, black pepper, and sometimes even licorice flavours. This varietal originated in Croatia and is genetically identical to Californian Zinfandel. It is not clear whether this grape travelled with the ancient Greeks who settled in the region thousands of years ago, or whether it arrived much later with the Greek-Albanian refugees who came to Puglia in the 15th and 16th centuries to escape the tyranny of the Ottoman Turks. The grapes were part of the dowry of Countess Sabini of Altamura when she married Don Tommaso Schiavoni-Trafuri of Manduria in 1881.

Perhaps the most interesting origin myth for Southern wine varieties belongs to Nero di Troia, an ancient variety that produces a well-balanced wine rich in tannins with beautiful hints of black currant and cherry. As usual, there is that familiar haze that obscures the grape's actual origins, but its name hints at a link to Greek heroes. A legend tells of the hero Diomedes leading a band of fugitives away from the destruction of Homer's mythic city of Troy. He sailed across the Adriatic and up the Ofanto river, and then settled on the Tavoliere plain. Using blocks from the ruined walls of Troy (conveniently brought with them aboard ship), Diomedes marked the boundaries of fields; according to agricultural historian Alfonso Germinario, one of these boundary markers (known as the Menhir of Canne) is still visible between the seaside towns of Barletta and Canosa north of Bari. Did Diomedes bring grape cuttings with him as well? New genetic research supports the idea that Nero di Troia not only originated in the Adriatic area but is closely related to other varietals from there. Perhaps most striking is the suggestion that its name comes from the Albanian city of Cruja, which locally translates as "Troy." Incidentally, the ideal *terroir* for this grape appears to be in northern Puglia near Foggia, and those legendary Diomedian fields.

13. The Amalfi Coast: The land where the lemon trees bloom

Now it's our turn, us poor ones, to have a share of riches, and it's the scent of lemons.
-Eugenio Montale

Even on the traffic-congested street in the small coastal town of Amalfi, Salvatore Aceto was easy to spot: he was wearing a bright green shirt with a comedic, tourist lemon striding across the front and "LEMON CREW" printed in bold letters across the back. Once he got our attention, and we were able to turn off the main road, we followed his small, white, electric car through the busy tourist district to the base of his lemon farm. Salvatore is a third-generation lemon farmer turned entrepreneur, and was excited to show us his farm, located on the steep slopes above. His new business venture, called the Lemon Experience, is the most recent chapter in the long story of lemons in southern Italy.

Lemons have a lengthy history in Italy, but are native to Asia (first grown in Assam in India, Burma and China). How and when they spread into the Mediterranean is difficult to figure out because of preservation. The decay of the outer seed coat makes lemons difficult to identify in archaeological sites, but new DNA techniques are making it possible to not only identify citrus more confidently, but also identify the different taxa. The earliest evidence of citrus in the Mediterranean comes from the 6th century BC necropolis site of Monte Sirai in southern Sardinia. The use of highly symbolic materials like beebread (pollen mixed with honey) and citrus for libations and offerings to the dead was revealed through chemical analysis of organic residues found in a wine jug. This, along with new DNA work, suggests that the Phoenicians and Punic traders may actually be responsible for some of this very early spread of lemons along the southern margins of Italy and the north coast of the Mediterranean (along with other things, like olive trees).

Citrus may have arrived in southern Italy by the first millennium BC. Pollen samples from the lagoon at the ancient city of Cumae (now Cuma-Fusaro near Napoli) revealed the presence of citrus in enough quantities to suggest that citrus trees may have been cultivated in southern Italy as early as 896-657 BC. Cumae was one of the earliest Greek colonies of *Magna Graecia* (greater Greece) and played a major role in the transfer of Greek cultural influence to Etruscan and Roman civilizations, so the potential of citrus groves here is fascinating in terms of understanding the movement of citrus through the Mediterranean. Evidence from Pompeii from both paintings and botanical remains suggests that lemons were present from the 3rd or 2nd century BC and were certainly being grown by the 1st century AD.

Frescos indicate that the lemon tree was an ornamental component of Roman gardens, often grown in pots. Beyond aesthetics, the earliest uses of lemons appear to be as therapeutics rather than food. In the 4th century BC the Greek philosopher Theophrastus reported that lemon fruit was used for bad breath and to preserve woolen cloth, while Pliny later talked of using lemons as antidotes for different poisons. The lemon's status as an ornamental and therapeutic item, rather than a culinary one, may have stunted its widespread adoption and cultivation, although presumably some time would have been required to breed lemons adapted to the environmental constraints of southern Italy; indeed, this remains the northern range of lemon cultivation outside of modern greenhouses.

Until very recently the Moors were credited with introducing lemons to Italy. While it is becoming increasingly obvious from archaeological evidence that lemons were introduced very early to southern Italy, they remained an ornamental curiosity until the southern peninsula was infused with Arab influence in the medieval period (Arabs arrived in Sicily in 827 AD and were in power there until 1061 AD when they were overthrown by Norman invaders.) The Arabs introduced many agricultural items: for the kitchen garden we see eggplant, spinach, pistachio, carob, and apricots; more broadly we see rice, sugarcane, cinnamon, and mulberry trees for silk production in Sicily. In fact, the Arabic word for lemon is *laymun*, similar to the Italian *limone*.

Not only did Arab cuisine cherish lemons as an acidic ingredient in food (witness Ibn Jamiya's book *The Treatise of the Lemon* written in 463 AD), it also introduced better technology to grow the fruit. This influence on the medieval landscape is captured in the common references made by northern Italians that described southern Italy as the "land where the lemon trees bloom." The earliest documentation of lemon gardens on the Amalfi Coast dates to the 11th century.

Demand for lemons really increased when it was discovered that lemon juice prevented and cured scurvy. This led to more intensified cultivation and organized trade of lemons beginning in the 16th century, at the zenith of the Age of Exploration. Ships arriving in the Mediterranean paid for lemons with precious cargo, including gold. By the 18th century, demand for lemons had increased significantly and farmers replaced less profitable crops like olive trees, vineyards and woodlots with lemons to meet the rising international demand. Farmers also developed new technologies to meet the ecological constraints of growing lemons in such a challenging environment.

Southern Italy: land of lemons

Lemons are central to the identity and integrity of Amalfi culture. Lemons are widely used in cooking, even their leaves are used to impart a special flavour. While visiting the Aceto's farm we enjoyed a smoked mozzarella that had been smoked in lemon leaves. Lemons have long been used as a medicine; the fruit itself is used, but the thick skins of the Amalfi lemon are full of oils that also pack a medicinal punch. They are a pharmacy disguised as a fruit: they are used as an antiseptic; for headaches; against flies and mosquitoes; can apparently treat bronchitis, liver failure, gout, kidney stones, nausea, and rheumatism; have antioxidant properties; and thwart scurvy. Small wonder that they have infiltrated the cuisine and soul of the region.

Because lemons are sensitive to cold climates, a few special varieties (*Sfusato Amalfitano* in particular) have evolved in response to the unique conditions of the Sorrentino peninsula along the Amalfi Coast. You cannot win any food from the steep- sided valleys without significant landscape modification; lemons are cultivated on stone-walled terraces which hug the narrow valley sides that fall away to the sea.

Many family farms (like the Acetos' farm) have been hard won. Southern Italy was largely a feudal economy until quite recently, and individuals and their families tended lemon gardens owned by wealthy landlords. In the Aceto family's case, having thirteen children during Mussolini's dictatorship in the 1930s qualified them for a special large family subsidy. The extra money, combined with the landowner falling on hard financial times, created the opportunity for the tenant farmer to become a landowner. This was amplified in 1968 when Salvatore's grandfather enlarged the plot to about twenty acres with a special low interest loan from the Italian state, part of land reform initiatives designed to help farmers buy their own land.

The lemons themselves are hard won too. Maintaining and harvesting the lemon groves of the Amalfi Coast requires huge amounts of human labour for a modest return. Traditional agricultural practices are still largely intact, meaning that most of these lemons are organic; animal manure is used for fertilizer, and because of the reduced light under the pergolas, weed growth is minimal so there is little need for herbicides. The result is lower production per hectare than elsewhere in Italy, which makes it difficult for these farmers to compete in the modern economy. The hope is that the superior quality and organic nature of this product gives these lemons added value for consumers.

Addressing the vulnerabilities of heritage agriculture

Keeping the lemon groves operational and even marginally profitable is a constant struggle. Integrating into the global economy has made it very difficult for small lemon farmers to compete with growers from Sicily and other countries. Argentinian lemons sell for 50 cents per kilogram in Napoli, but to cover his costs Salvatore has to sell his lemons for over 3 euros per kilogram; clearly, it is not possible to compete just on price, which is why he is focusing instead on quality. The overhead costs are significant and most come back to the challenges of farming in such an extreme landscape. The introduction of the euro did not help either since it raised the price of Italian exports, making it harder for small businesses to compete. On top of all that, the very landscape that has shaped and been shaped by these lemons can deliver a cruel blow to crops: 2014-15 was the worst season in twenty-five years and Salvatore's family farm lost 75 percent of their lemons. Today the land is more valuable for luxury tourism than boutique lemons, despite the fact that the lemons actually create much of the cultural draw for the peninsula, supplementing its natural beauty. Combined, these factors lead to the abandonment of gardens, as youth choose to leave the hard life of lemon growing behind in favour of an education and jobs in urban centres.

Salvatore's story really highlights this modern reality, and the challenges of maintaining Amalfi's lemon traditions. Like many, Salvatore left the lemon gardens and got his PhD in economics. He had a good job as an accountant in Napoli and was raising his family, when his father reminded him of the lemon juice that ran through his veins. His father implored him to remember his name, his identity, his heritage, all of which are tied to lemons, things he ultimately recognized he was disconnected from as he lived a good life with lots of money to spend but no connection to the land and his family. So in 2012 he returned to the farm. Taking a leap of faith and bringing his wife and daughters back to the farm would have been difficult; he left behind a well-paying job for an occupation that is truly a livelihood, an intersection of multiple generations of family, heritage, identity, and lemons. To survive in what many have dubbed "heroic agriculture," it was clear that a family has to operate as a unit, thinking and making decisions as one rather than as individuals. Three generations are currently involved in everything from the actual lemon farming to producing *limoncello* and courting tourists. He reflected that he is now in the real economy not just a virtual economy, and a recalibration of needs identifies that he doesn't really need that much extra money in a day: one euro for coffee with friends and one euro for his phone. We would all do well to pause and think about our lives through Salvatore's lens.

Salvatore does not need his degree in economics to see the many challenges that face the viability of Amalfi lemons in a modern market. In a sea of cheap imported lemons, these lemon gardens have a hard time breaking even, let alone making a profit. This might be manageable if you are farming lemons as a hobby, but not if this is your family's livelihood. A few initiatives are trying to address this hardship by highlighting the value of Amalfi lemons based on their quality and the integrated agricultural system that produces them. The recent Indicazione Geographica Protetta (GI) designation for the *Sfusato Amalfitano* variety (2001) recognizes the many values of lemon groves in this region, along with the vulnerabilities of maintaining this form of heritage agriculture. The specific microclimate, where cool breezes are trapped in the steep-sided valleys that cut perpendicular to the peninsula, imparts the taste of place that makes these lemons what they are. They are prized for their low acidity and delicate flavour. The hope is to appeal to a niche market and build direct relationships with customers throughout Europe to demonstrate the value of quality.

The greatest economic benefit identified by the FAO is tourism; thousands of tourists a year are drawn to the beautiful Amalfi Coast and its distinctive lemon gardens dripping down from the steep cliffs. The region's ties to tourism go back to the 17th century, when Sorrento became a stop along the Grand Tour; even then there was a connection between tourism and agriculture, and the region is ripe for reinvention with agritourism.

The Aceto family farm sells lemons and they make all sorts of lemon products like *limoncello* liqueur and lemon- infused soaps that are sold in their small, farm store and in Amalfi's tourist district. However, Salvatore quickly recognized it was no longer possible to live off only the profits of the lemon grove. Farmers must find other things to harvest from their farms, which is where agritourism comes in. The lemon tour is one way to diversify and create alternative revenue to survive, so the family puts on their matching lemon crew shirts, and walk people up and down their "enchanting" terraces, demonstrating the sweetness of their lemons by dramatically eating them like an apple (yes, skin and all!). A big, covered, seating area that overlooks the valley is a place to eat and enjoy cooking lessons led by Salvatore's wife. The family's "Lemon Experience" website promises tourists they will learn how to cook the "cult dishes of the Mediterranean cuisine" that they can then take home and "reproduce" for friends. *Limoncello* factory tours and tastings round out the experience that Salvatore hopes tourists will enjoy and write favourable reviews about on Trip Advisor.

And the reviews are fantastic. The smell of the lemon gardens and the buzz of bees amongst the fruit is incredible. This is authentic lemon farming, presented by the farmers themselves, which appeals to tourists wanting to connect with food traditions in more meaningful ways. Salvatore very clearly identified the vulnerabilities of traditional agricultural systems and their integration into a modern reality via agritourism enterprises. When you lose the majority of your crop because of weather, and cannot compete anyway because of the monstrous overhead of growing lemons in groves that cling to the side of steep valleys, you start to see how the approach is shaped by what the producer thinks the consumer wants. They do not need the matching shirts or theatrics. In commodifying his family's lemon gardens in hopes of saving them, Salvatore is presenting a brand that is carefully crafted to cater to the Tourist Gaze. The hope is that this juggling act saves not only the farm but retains a meaningful identity for Salvatore's family and the region.

Apart from cultural identity, maintaining the integrity of the lemon gardens is important from an environmental perspective as well. Lemon cultivation has created a landscape shaped by humans that not only sustainably provides food but also stabilizes the slopes with the construction of stone terraces. The deep roots of the lemon trees help to secure the steep slopes along a coastline that is susceptible to deadly landslides. The terraces prevent soil erosion and manage the rainwater, keeping what the trees need and draining the rest. Italy's leading geologists have sounded the alarm, estimating that if the lemon gardens disappear, the iconic landscape of the Amalfi Coast will follow, as landslides sweep the steep coastline into the Tyrrhenian Sea. In a world facing a future of more torrential rains thanks to climate change, these lemon gardens are a critical local conservation measure. When neighbours abandon their farms it creates enormous trouble for others in the valley trying to maintain their livelihood, not to mention those living below.

The interconnected natural and cultural values of this landscape have earned the lemon gardens (*giardini di limoni*) of the Sorrentino peninsula the GIAHS designation, a recognition by the FAO that they are a Globally Important Agricultural Heritage System. GIAHS designation is similar to UNESCO designations and others designed to raise awareness, build value, and promote conservation. As Angelo Amato, vice-president of the consortium for the protection of the Amalfi Coast lemon puts it, "*lemon farmers here are the sentinels of the environment.*"

The very nature of Amalfi lemons may also prove beneficial to the local economy. Lemon gardens are labour intensive, and maintaining the stone terraces and pergola structures, not to mention picking the fruit, could generate good jobs. These jobs would also be year round since lemons produce throughout the year, removing the need for seasonal labourers. These stable and sustainable jobs could be a good stimulus for the small towns of the Amalfi Coast, provided there is continued demand for the product.

Rejuvenation initiatives provide certification for Amalfi lemons and value the brand in a bid to maintain and build economic vitality. The Consortium for the Protection of the Amalfi Lemon (one of many Italian consortiums designed to protect "traditional foods") is a key ambassador to publicize and promote the "Amalfi lemon" as a living integrated component that helps makes the Amalfi Coast the UNESCO World Heritage site that it is. It also provides certification in tandem with the Indicazione Geographica Protetta (GI). However, according to Salvatore, the consortium also pressures farmers to increase yields (for more profit) by introducing irrigation, which may not be sustainable. The consortium also includes middlemen who warehouse and distribute the lemons (and profit from them). However, the Aceto family wants to maintain control over the distribution to see more of the final profit come back to the farm, similar to the premise of fair trade. Like so many other examples, these realities highlight the challenges of maintaining heritage, farming systems and foodways in a modern reality based on capitalism. As the saying goes, "When life gives you lemons, make lemonade." Never has this been more apt than for the lemon farmers of Amalfi.

Limoncello

It can feel a bit daunting to make your own version of Italy's incredible lemon aperitif. Online recipes offer conflicting instructions on how long to steep lemon rind. They make the whole process sound complicated (especially avoiding the white part of the peel so it doesn't impart a bitter flavour). Rosanna Denora makes *limoncello* effortlessly, and the results are delicious. Have fun trying this out in your own kitchen.

1L of pure alcohol (95% proof Everclear if you can find it. Vodka is a decent substitute.)

10 medium organic lemons

Simple sugar syrup

Directions:

Peel the lemons and place the rind in a container with the alcohol. Be sure that the lemons do not have wax on them. The most flavourful lemons that are seasonally available in North America are Meyer lemons. You can use a regular vegetable peeler, but try not to peel the white part of the rind as it will give the liqueur a bitter flavour. Steep for 3 days.

The amount of alcohol can be split in half to make a batch of regular *limoncello* and a batch of *crème limoncello*.

Simple sugar syrup:	Simple sugar syrup for *crème limoncello:*
750ml (3 cups) water	1L (4 cups) milk
300g (1 ½ cups) sugar	250g (1 ¼ cups) sugar
Boil and then let cool	Add 1-2 cinnamon sticks while boiling, then let cool

Strain the lemon rind from the alcohol and add the simple sugar syrup. Bottle in an airtight container. The best *limoncello* is served cold, so reserve a space in your fridge for this delicious after-dinner treat.

14. Lemons

Since the late 1700s, the Amalfi Coast has been known for its lemons. Wealthy travelers on the Grand Tour would come to marvel at the steep terraced farms tended by *"contadini volante,"* the "flying farmers," who spent their lives climbing the steep stairs to tend the gardens. The Aceto farm is typical of lemon gardens in the region. Lemons are grown 50 to 300 meters above sea level in a series of narrow stone-walled terraces that climb up the valleys running perpendicular to the coast. The lower part of the farm was built in the 1200s, and some of the trees in their gardens are 300 to 500 years old, a testament to the deep heritage of lemon farming on the Sorrentino peninsula. The fruit trees are customarily grown in *pagliarelle*, a technology developed in the mid-1800s made of straw and integrated into a chestnut-wood pergola; lemon gardens are also protected from the salty ocean winds by mat screens that act as windbreaks. These technologies are customized to the landscape, and in turn make this landscape--and the lemons grown within it--unique.

Terraces of lemons, some covered in green netting, step down the steep slopes to the seaside town of Amalfi.

Amalfi lemons hang from wooden pergolas. The stone retaining wall of the terrace is on the left.

The pergolas reduce the amount of sunlight that reaches the trees, slowing down the development of sugars and pigments in the lemon's rind; Luigi Aceto describes the advantage of the pergola: "*The rays of the sun penetrate under the roots so that the lemon is like a little baby in its cradle.*" And big babies they are: some lemons hanging from these structures weigh one kilogram each.

The lemons of the Amalfi Coast are a unique variety that has developed as a product of its environment. The *Sfusato Amalfitano* ("*Sfusato Amalfitano*") variety acquires a strong yet sweet flavour and a pale yellow colour. This fruit's zest is high in lemon oils, making it especially good for *limoncello*. The variety name "*fuso*" means spindle, referring to the shape of the lemons. There is one crop per year, but the lemon gardens display all stages of the lemon's life at once; the reduced light and temperature means that lemons flower late in the spring, starting in May when the harvest of fruit from the previous year begins.

Growing lemons on these farms is hard work. It is almost impossible to mechanize, so is demanding of human labour, with an infrastructure that is expensive to maintain. The white chestnut stakes of the pergolas need to be replaced every twelve years. This cannot be done any other way than with human labour; the 60 kilogram (132 lbs) logs must be carried up the steep steps of the terrace on human shoulders. The only mechanized component of the operation is a gondola system that carries crates of picked lemons down off the terraces, otherwise everything is done by hand. The stone retaining walls are generations old, and when they breach and need repair it costs thousands of euros. These are not overhead costs that lemon farmers in flatter landscapes of Sicily and other parts of Campania have to absorb; Amalfi lemon farmers will never be able to match the price of cheaper lemons from elsewhere, so value has to be defined differently.

Increasingly, value is being considered in terms of the quality of the lemons themselves, but also the contribution of lemon farms to the broader picture. Although traditional agricultural practices are still largely intact, many farmers are trying to increase their production by introducing chemical fertilizers, pesticides, and herbicides. While this may increase harvest in the short term, Salvatore feels this is short-sighted. Due to reduced light under the pergolas weed growth is minimal so there is actually little need for herbicides, and animal manure is an excellent, locally-sourced fertilizer. Keeping the farms organic should not only add to the superior quality and perceived value for consumers, but benefits the greater system as well.

This became obvious as we walked amongst Salvatore's lemon trees; at one point he stopped and put his finger to his lips. The pergolas were buzzing. *"Listen to the bees,"* said Salvatore, with a big smile. *"They work for me!"*

Pergolas require a good supply of chestnut wood so chestnut trees have been planted in the mountains of the peninsula. This maintains forests that are crucial elements of the integrated ecosystem and contribute to the broader economy.

129

Organic farming is essential for bee populations. Salvatore has been trying to convince neighbouring farmers that because of their excellent pollination ability keeping the bees happy actually amplifies harvests. This means keeping farms organic but also opening the netting that protects the lemons from hailstorms and heavy rains--but also keeps out the bees. The Aceto farm now has twenty-five hives; their bees pollinate their lemons and nearby gardens too, and Salvatore's predictions have come true. They also provide honey, which is sold in the farm shop as another source of income.

Salvatore's expertise in economics and marketing tells him he needs to cultivate direct relationships with customers to define the value of quality and include the human story in the brand. This is what the niche market wants, and gives him the most control over how his products are sold and who benefits. His family is part of the entire life history of their lemons, from seed to finished *limoncello* liqueur. Their story is a connection to history, a personal family one, but a deeper history of the region as well. More than that, it is a profound connection to a unique landscape that has shaped the *Sfusato Amalfitano* lemon and now depends on them for the future. Valuing the Amalfi lemon is now about so much more than a cherished ingredient.

15. Of Nuns and Pastries: Cooking up food traditions in God's kitchens

In 2014, on my first visit to Italy, my husband and I woke early with jet lag and, eager to explore, ventured into the nearby town of Altamura. Looking for a cup of coffee, we wandered into a local bakery. The pastries looked incredibly tempting, but having just had breakfast we declined. When our coffee was brought to us, two lovely domed pastries were delivered as well, on the house. These small domes had delicate points on the top and were dusted with icing sugar; fresh cream filling escaped from the base. Curious, I asked the woman the name of the pastry, to which she replied, *"tette di suore."* In 2014 my Italian was non-existent, but my background in French chimed in: it sounded like "tête," (or "head" in French). "Tête?" I asked, pointing to my head. *"No!"* She flushed, stepped back, and patted her chest. Ahhh, "nun's breasts"-- charades has never been so amusing.

Jean Anthelme Brillat-Savarin, the famous nineteenth-century French food writer, once noted that *"nunneries in the old days were veritable storehouses of the most delectable tidbits."* Across Europe monasteries made important contributions to gastronomy.[1] It is fairly well recognized that European and British monks were experts (and in some cases still are) in making ale, wine and cheese. What is less well known is that while monks excelled in these gendered tasks, nuns were equally busy in the kitchens of their cloistered monasteries growing herbs and making jams, confections, biscuits, and pastries.

When I think about nuns, sweet treats are not top of mind. A nun is a woman who belongs to a religious order and takes solemn vows of poverty, chastity, and obedience. A nun's life is one of humble sacrifice in deference to the sacrifices of Christ. The physical sacrifices serve to refocus an individual's mind, body, and spirit towards her dedication to God. The most extreme expression of this is when nuns live a cloistered life in a monastery. This physical and symbolic withdrawal from society to contemplate and serve God means that nuns are not allowed to leave the cloister, and visitors are only permitted in special areas. In this context, the idea of nuns living an isolated existence of piety and dedication to God, yet making mouth-watering (and often sexually suggestive) pastries, as well as maintaining many of Italy's pastry traditions, seems counter-intuitive. What gives?!

Perhaps it starts with some historical context. Sweets were important parts of seasonal celebrations, punctuating an otherwise unremarkable peasant diet of local and seasonal vegetables, legumes, and the ubiquitous serving of bread. For example, *panforte* was traditionally a Christmas sweet bread made by nuns, and *frutta di Martorana*, the realistic looking marzipan fruit treats that were given to children as presents from their dead relatives on All Souls Day (November 2), originally hailed from the Monastero della Martorana in the 12th century. But peasants didn't have access to the expensive exotic ingredients that define these sweets and pastries. Farmers could participate in alchemy of sorts, bringing the raw ingredients of flour and olive oil from their farms to the convents as patronage, and receiving pastries and sweets in return throughout the year. Additionally, until fairly recently, Italian households in the south did not have ovens (which created the need for communal bakeries), so it makes sense that nuns, with the social means to access sugar and spices, as well as the time to prepare delicious treats, were the master confectioners and pastry chefs. Convents and monasteries had something unique to offer their communities: pastries could maintain relationships with patrons who supported such religious

---

[1] While the English usage of the term monastery refers to monks, its original meaning, and its usage in Italian today, refers more generally to religious communities, which can include nunneries and convents. The monasteries referred to in this chapter are the enclaves of nuns.

establishments, but they were also something to sell to fund regular operating costs and charitable causes. Just as the European monopoly on cacao was shrewd economics for the Jesuits in the 17th century, the monopoly on exquisite pastries was a highly lucrative trade for monasteries. The products of monasteries and convents helped supplement the donations from their community and support from the Church to maintain their self-sufficiency.

Could the production of delicacies in part be a demonstration of will power and discipline, the ultimate expression of defying temptation to uphold the vows of devotion? In the 14th and 15th centuries, fasting and other forms of penitence were key elements of monastic life. They were integral to ecclesiastical ideology: the sins of gluttony and lust were never far away, especially for women. Across Europe, from at least the medieval period, women were considered slaves to their bodily appetites; for propriety's sake, appetite had to be controlled. Foods that were thought to stimulate the sensual rather than the moral nature of women were dangerous and to be avoided. This is one of the reasons that women were discouraged from eating much meat, a food thought to awaken carnal desires that is still, to this day, associated with masculinity. If the statistics on female sainthood are any indication, extreme austerities were considered a central aspect of holiness, and food practices were critical expressions of women's moral character. When I first started my inquiries about monastic pastry traditions, I wondered if making but not eating these voluptuous treats was a very clear expression of self-control; while this may be the case to some extent, it turns out that definitions of sacrifice and piety did not necessarily extend to the menus of Italy's convents. For centuries it was common practice for unmarried women in elite society to enter convents. This was often considered a better financial option for their families than an inferior marriage, and was a common way to preserve family finances in Catholic contexts. In 1552, one in eight elite women in Florence was part of a religious community, and such upper-class women did not leave their privileged taste in food at the monastery's gates. Leaving behind the life one knows to enter a religious community is difficult. Maybe this is why there was some flexibility in the interpretations of pious eating; in many cases convent food was remarkably similar to that of aristocratic households. According to Cristina Mazzoni, the convents of southern Italy of the 17th through 19th centuries were not serving the watery onion soup of peasants; they consumed larger quantities of food, and more expensive foods like eggs, almonds, and spices than most of the general public. In *The Physiology of Taste*, Brillat Savarin considers the apparent inconsistency between the supposed life of asceticism and the menus of devout monks and nuns. While many interpreted their vows in the extreme, perhaps they were exceptions. Eating good food can be justified as making the most of what God put on the earth for the specific use of humans. It would therefore be important to take advantage of these good things to intensify one's gratitude to God.

While many of the sweet treats were consumed by the nuns, a considerable amount was used to maintain critical connections with families and communities beyond the cloistered confines of the convent. The nuns' products were used as gifts to clergy and patron supporters of the convents. Venetian cloistered nuns of the 16th century regularly sent their families presents of sweets; interestingly, a 1596 source indicates that sweets accounted for half of the convent's food per year! Convents had large stocks of costly ingredients like sugar, honey, eggs, almonds, and exotic spices like cinnamon, nutmeg, and cloves that they received from wealthy supporters. As Cristina Mazzoni suggests, the time and energy invested to maintain these relationships by baking must have seemed a small price to pay to stay connected with the outside world. Indeed, when I visited a cloistered nunnery in Scala on the Amalfi Coast in 2014, a box of lemon biscotti was pressed into my hands as we left, a token of their thanks for the visit.

God's kitchens were busy places where nuns could use baking and confections as expressions of creativity, devotion, and pride. Pastries and treats were labour intensive, but they were also enjoyable to make (and eat) and provided a nice change of pace from the monotonous predictability of convent life. Cooking may also be a form of active meditation, busying the hands to free the mind to contemplate. Of course, this is not always the case; according to food historian Clifford Wright, *cassata*, the famous Sicilian sponge cake associated with Easter, was such a delicious distraction that in 1574 the diocese of Mazara del Vallo banned it from monastery kitchens during Holy Week because the nuns preferred baking and eating it to praying. Yet, for all the renouncing of secular realities, including rising above bodily needs to get closer to God, there is a domesticity and nurturing aspect to cooking and the kitchen; perhaps baking helps negotiate the compromises of a monastic life with more grace. Even more striking, the confections for which individual convents were famous were sources of pride for nuns. Just because they were cloistered did not mean they had lost their competitive spirits; they spared no expense when it came to ingredients to both uphold the high quality of their products and impress the cardinals and abbots who regularly visited.

Monasteries were known for their specialties, which often reflected both deep historic traditions and the products of the local landscape. The lingering tastes of the Moors are everywhere in southern Italy, but Sicilian pastries and confections are ground zero. Cane sugar and a variety of fruits such as apricots were first introduced in the late 800s by the Arabs, who also encouraged the increased use of almonds as sweeteners and thickeners. Arabic flavours of saffron and cinnamon merged with pre-existing ones to create the distinctive pastries that are still made today. Because of the climate, sheep were the favoured dairy animal in the southern part of the Italian peninsula, and so it is tangy sheep's milk ricotta (sweetened with powdered sugar) that fills the centres of *sfingi, cassata,* and *cannoli,* imparting these signature Sicilian pastries with their distinctive taste. In Palmero alone, there were twenty-one monasteries renowned for their pastries and confections in the 18th and 19th centuries. The poet Giovanni Meli hints at the scope of special sweet treats made by religious orders in southern Italy in his poem *Li cosi duci de li battii* (The Sweet Things from the Abbeys). Examples include *cassata* from Valverde in Palermo, *cannoli* from Saint Catherina in Palermo, and *bocconcini* ("sweet morsels") from the Abbey of the Holy Rosary in Palma Montechiaro. In Napoli, controversy surrounds the exact convent origins of *sfogliatella*; convents on the Amalfi Coast and Naples have both laid claim. Regardless of whether these delicious pastries originated on the Amalfi Coast and diffused to Napoli or vice versa, what is clear is that in and around Napoli in the 17th century (and possibly earlier) convents were famous for one or more sweets made by their nuns, be it pastries, sour cherries in syrup, or preserved pears. Maintaining the brand was essential to retaining loyal customers, and most of the recipes for these sweet treats were closely guarded secrets to ensure that other monasteries did not dilute the brand by producing "inferior" pastries. Since cloistered nuns have very little interaction with the external world, keeping these recipes safely inside the convent walls was not particularly challenging; *sfogliatella* may represent a breach here, with a recipe smuggled out and compromising the supremacy of its original producers!

The psychology of sacrifice, devotion, and denial is complex. This is evident in the context of convents, where women exchanged the ability to move freely through the secular world for a closer connection with God. As Brides of Christ, these women renounced bodily pleasures, yet food seems to occupy an interesting gray area as a source of sanctioned titillation and covert fantasy. The Song of Songs, scripture from the Old Testament, hints at the similarity between the enjoyment of sweetness and sexual pleasure; how then to make sense of the examples of convent treats inspired by erogenous body parts? *Fedde*, pistachio-flavoured pastries, linguistically refer to and physically resemble buttocks. The most popular version is called *fedde del cancelliere (*"chancellor's buttocks"), maybe suggesting either suppressed female desires, or more subversive, gentle derision.

Sicily's most famous dessert, *canolli,* originates from a convent in Caltanissetta. As one of many phallic symbols associated with Carnival, a

St. Agatha is the patron saint of breast cancer survivors.

fertility celebration, these long, cream-filled pastries offered protection against evil spirits. Other well-known pastries originally made in monasteries are *Mimi di Virgini,* also known as *tete di suore* or "Saint Agatha's breasts," that traditionally were consumed during the feast of Saint Agatha on February 5. Agatha's story is one of Christian celibacy and the rejection of paganism, and her subsequent martyrdom for these values. When the young Agatha snubbed a Roman suitor in AD 251 to honour her commitment to Christ, he punished her by cutting off her breasts. This part of the story, apparently the most significant, is immortalized in breast-shaped pastries filled with cream. Never mind that Saint Paul miraculously healed her breasts, or that she ultimately died a martyr when she was tortured and killed on burning coals; the part of her story immortalized in food memory are her breasts. Paintings of Saint Agatha generally depict her with her breasts on a platter that many argue resembles a cake plate. Are Saint Agatha's breasts edible icons of sexual sadomasochism? It is interesting that all of these pastries encourage putting these body parts in one's mouth; the symbolism here (in the context of celibate nuns) is eyebrow-raising to say the least.

Looking more closely at the origins of these specific convent pastries, it becomes clear that these symbols may be less about erotica and more about fertility. There remains a deep connection with pre-Christian traditions that included various offerings to the gods in shapes of breasts and genitalia, a connection that can still be seen in the similarities between Christian religious holidays and pre-Christian festivals. The familiar Easter eggs recall pagan festivals celebrating the arrival of spring, valuing eggs as potent symbols of new life. Incorporated into Christianity, Easter eggs are explained as representing both Christ's emergence from the tomb and his resurrection; the timing of Easter and pre-Christian spring fertility festivals is likely not a coincidence. Christianity found it easier to adopt existing celebrations rather than to eliminate them. *Scarcella*, a traditional Pugliese pastry that is made at Easter for children, is a cake shaped like a hen, basket, or ring with a whole egg (shell and all) on top, encased in a cross of dough.

The concentration of these symbols in Roman Catholic pastry traditions in southern Italy may actually have great antiquity. Beginning in the 8th century BC, the southern peninsula hosted a number of Greek colonies known as *Magna Graecia*, who brought their religious traditions (and other things like grapes and wine culture) with them. Despite the region and its peoples being conquered by the Romans in the 3rd century BC, and later being influenced by orthodox Christianity of the Byzantine Empire, many pre-Christian religious symbols prevail. Demeter, Greek goddess of the harvest, was responsible for the fertility of the earth and reigned supreme; numerous spring festivals were held in her honour. Part of the annual Thesmophorai festivals included special honey and sesame seed cakes shaped like female genitals. These cakes, called *mylloi*, were carried around in honour of the goddess, and clearly made their way into Sicilian food traditions. To ensure a successful wheat crop, the goddess needed a husband, and fertility rites represented the consummation of the marriage and promise of new life.

The connection between sexually-allusive foods and agricultural rites is understandable. As other trappings of these pre-Christian rituals have waned in the last 1500 years, the enduring presence of the symbolism in food that is now firmly associated with monasteries seems surprising. Rather than just erotica, these pastries may in fact represent religious syncretism, representations of very old rituals and symbols that were absorbed into Christianity in regions where the ancient Greeks had a lasting influence.

Other histories mixed into these pastries include the Arab influence felt most strikingly in the south. Arabs arrived in Sicily in AD 825 and for several centuries the island was the primary Muslim stronghold in the region, with limited, localized, and short-lived states in places like Bari, on the shores of the Adriatic in what is now the province of Puglia. In addition to the new ingredients that they brought with them, they also endowed the region with a variety of pastry recipes that until recently were only made in monasteries. For example, *Luna di Maometto* (Mohammed's Moon) is a rich pastry shaped like the Islamic crescent. *Strufoli* from Napoli, delicious deep-fried dough balls covered in honey and flavoured with citrus zest, are similar to many Middle Eastern confections. This legacy of Arab influence dating back twelve hundred years was absorbed into medieval convent life and remains a

Christmas specialty; today *strufolli* are either made at home or purchased from bakeries as important holiday treats.

Nuns and pastries in Altamura

Not so long ago there were many religious communities in Altamura, all located in the winding narrow streets of the old town, and integrated into the community in many ways. Monasteries provided the funds to build Altamura's communal bread ovens, and then leased them to bakers, who would pay in money and bread, thus putting food on the tables of the clergy. The names of these bakeries refer to the patron saints of the particular founding churches. For example, Pino's business (see Chapter 18) is still called Antico Forno di Santa Caterina (St. Catherine). Not far from Pino's cavernous bread oven is the church of Santa Chiara and its adjoining monastery. Monasterio di Santa Chiara also highlights the modern history of religious communities and the use of food as social (and hard) currency. Since 1682 it has offered education and training to local girls, become known for its embroidery (which the nuns would do for a fee), produced the sacred hosts used at mass, and made pastries. This is where Tonio's great-aunt was a cloistered nun. He remembers taking olive oil, wine, and durum wheat flour from their farm to the monastery as a child, and putting it on the rotating table that maintained the seclusion of cloistered residents, the shadowed figure of a sister visible through the grill. In return they got pastries on special holidays. Typical pastries from Altamura are almond based. The nuns made a wide variety of *pasticceria fresca* (fresh bakery) items, such as the domed *"tette di suore"* pastries filled with custard or crème, and sometimes topped with a cherry, and *pasticceria secca* (dried bakery) products, like almond paste cookies, or cookies topped with sliced almonds. Many of these show broad similarities with other monastic pastries of the south.

Social and economic changes that started in the late 19th century, the consequences of Unification and the Industrial Revolution which encouraged people to move out of poor southern communities to find work, compromised the large social networks that had worked together through a mutual sense of obligation. Large extended families began to fracture as people moved away. Increasingly, convents could no longer rely on food products as valued social currency and needed to find sources of income for financial self-sufficiency. Pastries and confections were now not only used as gifts but also sold as part of a profitable business.

Despite being repositories for food traditions for centuries, Italy's religious communities have faced the challenges of changing social dynamics and a modern world, and these traditions have eroded since World War II.

Monastery populations have withered; Monasterio di Santa Chiara had thirty nuns in the 1990s, but now there are only seventeen. Not only are religious community populations in decline, but the new generation of nuns is not as interested in pastry making as a way to connect with the broader community, preferring other contributions that seem more socially important than baking. Access to expensive ingredients and changing markets for selling pastries are also problems. The sense of community

Sisters from the Monastero delle Clarisse di Altamura, 1982 (courtesy of Pasticceria Monastero Santa Chiara Altamura)

charity has waned, and few producers are bringing ingredients to convent doors. State tax provisions once supported religious communities, but now individuals can choose where to direct part of their tax money from a list of worthy options; more competition among religious communities means less money. People now make their own pastries and cookies, or, increasingly, buy cheap packaged ones provided by the industrial food system. Nuns cannot compete, leaving them in the dust.

Historically, much of the nuns' success lay in maintaining the high quality and supremacy of particular pastry "brands". The monopoly crumbled as recipes and names for many monastic items were sold to business ventures in the 1950s, a time when many of these products were considered outdated, and convents and monasteries lacked the vision or resources to develop commercial ventures of their own. In 1989, the word *monastère* ("from a monastery or convent") was trademarked to promote and protect the authenticity of thousands of European products of monastic origin. Best known are Trappist products in terms of Belgian beer: to use the term Trappist, products must be made in abbeys under the supervision of Trappist monks of the Cistercian order.

In 2015, a new bakery opened in Altamura that celebrates the monastic tradition of pastries as part of its entrepreneurial identity. Old traditions are reimagined in a contemporary context in Pasticceria Monastero Santa Chiara, a sleek modern business in a building across the street from the church and monastery of Santa Chiara. The building is owned by the monastery, and according to Michael, the bakery's manager, one of the nuns continues to keep an eye on the work in the kitchen. The bakery advertises its use of traditional recipes from the nuns (it is not clear what kind of financial arrangement this entails, although the owner is related to the bishop, which can't hurt) and in celebrating the tradition, is using it as a point of distinction from other bakeries in town. While this might be considered opportunistic marketing, it brings this story into the modern fabric of Altamura, and celebrates these traditions so they are not completely forgotten.

While it would be romantically satisfying to see a nun in this bakery's kitchen, black habit flowing as she pipes crème fraiche into fresh pastries or loads trays of almond cookies into the industrial oven, her absence reflects the reality of monastic contributions in a modern world. Modern nuns do not want to be baking when there are so many other contributions that are considered more significant. Pasticceria Monastero Santa Chiara is an interesting place to think about the meaning of authenticity, and how identity and representation are always carefully crafted for an audience. Would it be more authentic to entice nuns back into the kitchen for the sake of photographs and fulfilling the expectations of customers? Certainly nuns are challenged to maintain their relevance in modern communities, but does the fact that nuns are no longer actively making these pastries make this bakery inauthentic? The tradition is now a story rather than a practice, but perhaps keeping the story alive dignifies the centuries-old heritage of pastry making in Italy's religious communities and maintains this connection to community and history in a way that is meaningful in the 21st century.

16. Almonds

Almonds (*Prunus dulcis*, syn. *Prunus amygdalus*) are native to Central Asia and the Middle East and may be one of the earliest domesticated trees. These fruit trees are closely related to cherries and peaches (their pits are incredibly similar), but while the size and flavor of these other fruits drove their domestication, with almonds the artificial selection shaped the seed, which is encased in the kernel in an otherwise inedible fruit (called a drupe). Wild almond trees are found in Armenia and the Levant (modern Syria, Jordan, Lebanon, Israel), which suggests that they were first domesticated in this broad region, but the specifics are still not very well understood. What is interesting about wild almonds is that they are toxic; like other members of the *Prunus* genus such as cherries and peaches, the kernels contain cyanide.

Eating even a few handfuls in one sitting can be fatal! The domestication of almonds began with the selection of sweet almonds, which do not have this poisonous trait. The archaeological record shows that the first domesticated almonds appeared in the Early Bronze Age (3000-2000 BC) in modern Jordan. Almonds imported from the Levant accompanied the Egyptian king Tutankhamun to the afterlife in his tomb (1325 BC).

The mention of almonds in the Old Testament is further proof of the antiquity of this domesticate in the Middle East. In the Book of Genesis the almond is described as "among the best of fruits." In the Hebrew Bible almonds symbolize watchfulness and promise because the trees flower early in the spring. In Christianity almond branches are a symbol for the virgin birth of Jesus. For the Romans almonds were a fertility charm. This was likely incorporated into Easter celebrations, which are spring rituals of fertility and rejuvenation. Along with Easter eggs, almond pastries and confections were standard fare in Sicily and the southern Italian peninsula.

According to the Roman writer Columella (AD 1), almonds are well suited to the "raw, hot and arid lands" of the Mediterranean basin, and so were spread fairly easily by either the Phoenicians or the Greeks. We cannot be sure when they first arrived on the Italian peninsula, but they were known by the first century BC. Both Cato the Censor and Virgil write about them. Evidence of nuts buried at Pompeii indicates that they were being consumed there in AD 79 when Vesuvius erupted and the city was destroyed. One of the more unusual comments about almonds comes from Alexis Soyer's nineteenth century survey of ancient European foods: the Romans believed that you only had to eat five or six almonds to *"acquire the ability of drinking astonishingly!"*

Almonds in Puglia

The first historic evidence of almonds in Puglia also date to the first century BC. Pliny the Elder tells us that there were two cultivars of almond grown around Taranto, both a hard-shelled and a soft-shelled variety. The region was so well known for its almonds that they became the source of an insult: in the 4th century AD Macrobius writes that the term "soft shell" was used as a reference to the weak character of Taranto inhabitants.

Historic records are scant following the fall of the Roman Empire and the medieval period, but by the 16th century it becomes clear that large almond orchards had spread to the province of Bari, and by the late 1800s cultivation was extensive and carefully managed. There were forty-six different varieties being grown in the area of Trani in Puglia; these were

Dozens of varieties of almonds continue to be grown on small Pugliese farms, often just for family use. These ones have an intense amaretto flavour.

mostly hard shelled, sweet kernel varieties, although four bitter kernel varieties are known from the region as well. The dry, calcium-rich soils and climatic conditions in about a hundred kilometer range from Bari are particularly well suited to almonds; at the peak of industrial production in the mid-1930s over eighty percent of Pugliese almonds were grown in this area.

Although almonds have a lengthy history in Puglia, the scale of cultivation has experienced both boom and bust. In the early 1900s European vineyards suffered from a devastating pest epidemic; a tiny aphid-like insect had a taste for grapevines, and a great number of vineyards were destroyed. In Puglia, this meant that farmers abandoned their vines in favour of olives and almonds, proven winners in the poor soils of the region. By the 1930s, almond exports were key to Pugliese economics, and with no other real competitors the relatively low yield of almonds was not a significant problem. However, after World War II the California almond industry found its feet and quickly offered stiff competition. Its irrigated almond orchards produced higher yields (10-15 times the Pugliese yield according to one report), and their production costs were lower. By the late 1950s farmers in Puglia were once again changing their crops to align with the market; almonds were uprooted and vineyards were replanted. By the 1960s the almond industry was in steady decline and by the year 2000 only about 25 percent of the area around Bari that had been growing almonds before World War II was still in production.

The use of almonds in Pugliese food traditions likely reflects a combination of historic Sicilian influences and local availability. Almond culture is generally associated with Sicily, and this is yet another example of the culinary legacy of the Arabs. Sicily was an Islamic state from AD 827-1072 (and interestingly, Bari was the centre of the short-lived Islamic Emirate of Bari from AD 847-871). After the Normans conquered Sicily in the late 11th century, their kingdom extended all the way to central Italy. This likely explains the spread of Arab-influenced foods and flavours via the Norman-Sicilian monasteries on the peninsula. A number of these items, like lemons and almonds, predated the arrival of Arabs in Sicily in the 800s, but the Arabs emphasized these ingredients and introduced new agricultural innovations (in this case likely orchard design and grafting techniques) that made them more successful and plentiful. After that, supply and demand fueled one another.

Puglia's cuisine is characterized by its use of local ingredients; in the case of sweets and desserts this means durum wheat, olive oil, and almonds. Almond paste (*pasta di mandorle*) is a common filling in pastries, and sliced almonds are often used as decoration. Although it is hard to reconstruct much of Byzantine period cuisine, they are remembered for their sweet tooth. Cookies similar to the following recipe were common (except for the vanilla, an ingredient that did not arrive in the region until the 1600's) because of their long shelf life. They were a standard product of monasteries throughout the southern Italian peninsula, and could very well have graced the dinner tables of the medieval period.

Almond Biscotti
(recipe adapted by Dale Mosher)

¾ cup whole almonds
3 eggs
1 tsp / 4 g vanilla extract
¼ tsp / 1 g almond extract
2 cups / 400 g unbleached flour
7/8 cup / 200 g sugar
1 tsp / 4 g baking soda
pinch of salt

Bake nuts in a preheated 350 degree F oven for 8-10 minutes until golden and then let cool. Toasting deepens the flavour and makes the nuts easier to chop.

Chop nuts in a food processor, or hand chop into thirds or smaller. (If the nuts are too big, they interfere with slicing the dough.) In a small bowl whisk together eggs and extracts for about 1 min. In a separate bowl stir together flour, sugar, baking soda and salt. Add egg mixture to flour mixture and stir together. While there is still a bit of flour showing add the chopped nuts. Mix thoroughly with your hands. Divide dough in half.

On a silicone mat or a greased and floured baking sheet, pat dough into 2 logs about ½ inch thick, 1½ inches wide, 12 inches long, about 2 inches apart. Bake in the centre of a 300 degree F oven for 40 minutes or until golden and firm to the touch.

Remove and place on a rack for 5 minutes. Reduce oven to 275 degrees F. Place logs on a cutting board. With a serrated knife slice a small piece off each end of the log (samples for the cook) and slice the logs diagonally about ¾ inch thick. Lay the slices flat on the baking sheet and return to the oven for 10 minutes. Remove and flip over the cookies and bake 10 minutes more.

Cool and store in a tightly covered tin. Makes about 2 dozen. Note these biscotti are very firm and best eaten after dunking in a coffee or glass of wine.

17. Tradition Does Not Exist

Tradition is the illusion of permanence.
-Woody Allen

When travelers visit new places they are often in search of an "authentic experience." While this may mean a variety of different things, authenticity is often synonymous with definitions and expectations of "tradition." The Oxford Dictionary tells us that "authenticity" is of undisputed origin and not a copy; genuine; something made or done in the traditional or original way. But what is this "original?" Authentic to whom, and based on what criteria? Is Italian food in America still authentic? Can there only be one authenticity? Or can we accommodate multiple, parallel ones?

During the Age of Enlightenment, European philosophers and thinkers contrasted the concept of modernity with the concept of tradition, all in the context of progress. This contributes to the popular definition of tradition as "holding on to a previous time," and when considered this way it can stagnate culture. This romantic construction turns vibrant culture, ever changing in response to stimuli like history, environment, and technology, into static artifacts of history. To be authentic seems to suggest something that does not change, and the potential outcome is an unrealistic (dare I say "inauthentic") reflection of a place, product, or people. This is problematic, and a circular argument.

Matera offers an interesting example of how ideas of "traditional" and "modern" have been cast as opposites, defined by and in relation to each other. Because the *sassi* life was branded a disgrace and "national shame" in the 1950s modernity was offered up as a shiny opportunity to be progressive. Former inhabitants of the *sassi* were encouraged to keep their gaze fixed squarely ahead and to embrace modern lifestyles--at the expense of many elements of their traditional identities. It is ironic that the rebranding of Matera today, in the limelight of the UNESCO World Heritage status bestowed in 1993, celebrates the peasant identity that was the "traditional" so demonized in the 1950s. The contemporary identity of Matera, one shaped by the Chamber of Commerce, and expected by tourists, is that of the peasant inhabitants of the "*sassi* city." While this nostalgic version of tradition works well for the tourist industry, and has fueled powerful examples of cultural rejuvenation, the non-peasant reality is not included in this version of "traditional"; the higher classes that have long inhabited Matera and contributed to its history are not very visible in this carefully crafted, contemporary identity. It is hard indeed to present a real identity that tourists also agree is authentic and traditional.

A more useful way to think about tradition begins with etymology. The word "tradition" itself derives from Latin *tradere*, literally meaning "to transmit," to hand over, an inheritance. This is also the root of the word "trade," the movement and exchange of ideas and material between multiple stakeholders. In this sense, tradition is a moving target, something that involves both producer and consumer as actors in a dynamic transaction. So tradition is defined by all participants in a dynamic way that defies a single meaning or characterization.

A tradition will change in response to context. New knowledge and technologies get infused with these practices and thus are dynamic reflections of living cultural heritage. A Messors participant was a bit disappointed to see a microwave in the *masseria* kitchen; apparently this modern kitchen gadget eroded the sense of eating traditional food. There was also surprise that we were eating store-bought, mass-produced pasta, bursting the dreamy illusion of a *nonna* painstakingly making pasta by hand for us every day. Humans have always embraced new technologies, customizing them and making them their own to be efficient, or successful, or just fashionable! What does not change is the link with the land. Even when you introduce a new variety of olives, grapes, or wheat, it is the environment that decides how the plant will grow and adapt, which in turn shapes the characteristics of the resulting oil, wine, or bread. This regional quality of food, which is not homogenized like so much of our industrial food system, but rather is preserved and celebrated as an expression of place is *terroir*. The only thing that doesn't change is the connection to the land; *this* is tradition.

Traditions also change in response to influences. Outsiders may define Italian food in very general terms, with items such as pasta, tomato sauce, espresso coffee, and specialty chocolates coming to mind. All of these are testaments to historic influences that brought new ideas and ingredients to the Italian peninsula. Of this list, only pasta, likely introduced by the Arabs in the 1200s, was heartily welcomed when it first arrived. All the other "authentic" Italian items were eyed with mistrust when they first arrived in Europe. The tomato was considered vile and poisonous; tomato sauces only really started to become popular 150 years after the fruit's arrival. Coffee, the "wine of Arabia" that first arrived in Italy in the early 1600s from the Turkish Empire, was associated with Islam and described by many concerned Christians as a "*hellish black brew*" invented by Satan. It was only after Pope Clement VIII cheated Satan by baptizing the beverage (and thus making it spiritually safe to drink) that coffee culture spread up and down the peninsula. And chocolate? Before becoming a sweet treat, chocolate was an elite beverage with the reputation for being an excellent vehicle for sorcery because it disguised the taste of poison. The potential for bewitched chocolate drinks to spread supernatural illness or even murder rivals led to much suspicion. Perhaps these fears were not unfounded; Pope Clement XIV was murdered in 1774, and most pointed to poison in his chocolate drink as the culprit. It seems clear that a dynamic definition of tradition is quite useful.

At issue here is representation: who is determining what is traditional, and what is not? It has a lot to do with power and voice. Like corn, pasta was originally a peasant food in many parts of southern Italy. When access to fresh vegetables and meat were compromised in Napoli markets under the reign of the Spanish, diets underwent a profound transformation towards carbohydrates, with pasta as king. We think of pasta as quintessentially Italian, but it is not a unified history. Noodles were introduced to southern Italy by the Arabs, who were influenced by their economic interactions with Asia. Dried noodles were produced on an industrial scale because they were cheap, travelled easily, and lasted a long time, contributing to the widespread popularity of the food item. This was once denigrated as the food of the poor, yet today is proudly represented as integral to Italian food identity. The same can be said of pizza, another iconic food born in Napoli's slums that has made the transition from poverty food to being nominated to UNESCO's list of intangible cultural heritage in 2016. We can now start to understand the assertion that "tradition" does not exist, certainly not in a static, "original" sense.

Promoting tradition through certification

As the Greek philosopher Heraclitus famously said, *"change is the only constant in life."* The challenge becomes accommodating more recent changes while still allowing them their place as authentic components of tradition. In Europe, this is complicated by the recognition of Geographic Indication of Origin Protection as a measure to preserve the integrity of food cultures and regional identities. The European Union has legislated a variety of designations for 'traditional specialties" that cover a wide variety of products such as wines (e.g., Champagne), cheeses (e.g., Roquefort), and meats (e.g., Parma ham). *Pane di Altamura* is the only bread in Europe with GI Protection, earning the designation in 2003. For bread to bear the PDO (Protected Designation of Origin) certificate with a small paper disk pressed into the crust and be called *Pane di Altamura*, *"the entire product must be traditionally and entirely manufactured (prepared, processed and produced) within the specific region and thus*

A special mixing machine with braccia tuffanti ("diving arms") mimics the motion of kneading by hand that is required to satisfy DOP rules. Each batch, which makes 80 loaves, requires 40 minutes of kneading in this machine.

acquire the unique properties of the [*Murgia Plateau*]." A list of strict conditions must be met. The bread can include only four ingredients in specified quantities: durum wheat flour Senatore Cappelli from the immediate vicinity of Altamura, *lievito madre* (mother yeast), hard local water, and sea salt. A standard rotating mixer won't do here; the dough must be lovingly mixed and kneaded in a machine that replicates the actions of a woman's arms. Although the most traditional bread will be baked in a wood oven, a gas oven is also permissible, but the crust must be no less than 3 mm thick and the crumb must have uniform air pockets, indicating the proper leavening of the natural yeast.

Commercially speaking, in the modern reality of capitalism and global markets where producers and consumers live worlds apart, it is important to have mechanisms to protect products from adulteration and "impersonation" (like 100 percent pure Italian olive oil for example). This ensures that producers can maintain their traditional foodways that are critical economically and an expression of identity. But certification is a bit hollow, often based on a farmer's paperwork or a producer's ability to pay for the credential. In quantifying and defining the conditions of authenticity, GI protection leaves little room for the living expression of tradition as we move into the future. If consumers learn how to taste the bread, the wine, the cheese, the oil, and how these products are made, they can certify for themselves, which is how it has always been. A shepherd only has a market for food that tastes good; bad food doesn't sell, and in this way consumers have always been the inspectors and certification body of food traditions. Again, this promotes the concept of tradition as a dynamic entity that requires the participation of all players in its creation and maintenance.

I think that GI designation can be viewed as a form of holistic conservation that recognizes tradition as the ongoing relationship between landscape and people, with food as an important conduit. In the case of Altamura bread, the DOP story began in the 1980s when there was a significant increase in the importation of grain from places like the Canadian prairies to meet demand. Demand has outstripped national supply for generations, and even Mussolini's Battle of the Grain in the 1930s could not deliver self-sufficiency. Imported wheat depressed the price of local durum wheat, so a movement driven by farmers and bakers crystalized to create more value for local bread and keep the price for local grain higher. The designation protects this local variety of wheat in a global economy of cheap, imported wheat, and helps to keep the price of local wheat at 10 euros per 100 kilograms, more than the standard price for wheat.

Having DOP status maintains demand for locally-produced grain. And maintaining demand for local wheat is a mandate to protect the landscape in which it is grown, including agricultural land, waterways, and the air. So, just as you can't understand the food without understanding the landscape, you can't enjoy the food if the landscape isn't there to support it. DOP status and similar designations dignify the cultural knowledge and can help make professions like shepherding and cheese making viable options for youth, which in turn facilitate and encourage the transmission of oral traditions to maintain the great wealth of potential; individuals can choose to do with it what they will. This integrated approach to conservation considers culture and the environment together, recognizing that neither exists in isolation, and neither can be "authentic" if the relationship is severed. Perhaps GI designation then preserves tradition not of certified products themselves but the possibilities of the landscape to continue to offer ingredients (both tangible and intangible) that fuel creative cultural traditions. This will allow for a future where *Pane di Altamura* tastes the same as it does now--similar to what Horace described in his poetry 2,000 years ago—because of the *terroir*. But it will also maintain these ingredients for novel re-imaginings and additions that may reflect new immigrant influences from Africa and India. These breads can be enjoyed side by side, as the tastes of dynamic culture.

Fitting traditional foods into modern molds: artisan food and EU regulations

The incredible array of European designations like DOP speak to the desire to maintain these "traditional foods" as ingredients of local identity, especially important in a modern world where homogenization lurks in every corner of the global industrial food system. What is difficult with this dynamic definition of tradition is figuring out how to balance celebrating change

Bright poppies hide amongst the nodding heads of wheat on the Murgia Plateau.

without forcing change to the point that it has a really negative impact. The power dynamics of modernity can really threaten traditional foods and the people who make them.

A key component of the European Union's sweeping set of food regulations is the Hygiene Package. The primary objective of these policies is that food that reaches consumers be safe--which everyone would agree is important. At issue here is the determination of food safety. As disconnected consumers in a large, industrial food system, we must turn to state inspectors and regulations to do what consumers did not all that long ago when they had direct relationships with the people producing their food. In a global system we may not even know where on Earth our food comes from, let alone the conditions it was grown and processed in; the personal, geographic, and psychological bonds of trust are gone, so we are forced to trust the state policies. Unfortunately, these are pretty blunt instruments, designed to address food safety issues of large-scale operations, many of which are not even an issue for small-scale, conscientious producers. These regulations can change the food we eat, and be extremely hard for small producers to meet.

Microbes have been cast as Public Enemy Number One by the Hygiene Movement, which emerged in the late 1800s with champions like Louis Pasteur, who brought us pasteurization. In the context of rapidly expanding urban centres where diseases were rampant, new standards of hygiene became synonymous with modernity. Pasteurizing milk was introduced to address a wide range of diseases like typhoid, diphtheria, and tuberculosis. Many now suggest that these diseases were made worse because of the scale of operations; animals confined in filthy, manure-filled pens, workers with dirty hands, diseased animals, and contaminants in milk pails were certainly a recipe for disaster. And pasteurization has clearly addressed public health issues, most significantly infant mortality rates. But what is hard to evaluate in the din of the hygiene paradigm is that when production happens at a small-scale operation, with producers who are part of every aspect of the production chain, the disease risks of drinking raw milk products is minimized. When producers know their individual animals and milk them by hand, for example, they are fine tuned to the health of their animals. When there is a short period of time between milking and the transformation of the milk into cheese, the development of deadly pathogens is minimized. Aging cheeses and curing meats for many months allows the good microbes to win the battle against the nasty ones.

But hygiene rules have ushered in more sanitized products of modernity that lack much of the flavour of real, "traditional" food. Take the classic Swiss Emmenthal cheese, for example, the stereotypical cheese known for its large and numerous holes. These holes are due to bacteria that emit a gas as they digest part of the cheese in the aging process, leading to bubbles. New rules require the milk to be pasteurized, and with fewer gas-emitting bacteria in the process Emmenthal cheese has smaller and less numerous air bubbles. When this and other sanitized components of modern production enter the equation, the soul of the product is changed, a compromise in the name of food safety.

It may be a more aesthetic difference, an easy compromise to swallow, but many of these modern policies have negative effects for small producers. Shepherds require various certifications to produce milk and cheese. Meeting the requirements for the animals' health seems to be fairly easy to accomplish, but small shepherds have a very hard time getting their premises up to inspection standards that will be approved by the local food authorities to enable commercial sale of products. Making cheese over an open fire, in cramped spaces with blackened surfaces that have collected the soot of production for decades is quite different from the stainless steel and white ceramic tile of modern cheese-making operations.   From a personal observation, there is a different feel to small-scale operations that cannot afford to upgrade to meet the rules. In these cases shepherding is a way of life instead of merely a job; upgrading requires a scale that is untenable for small producers with small profit margins.

Modern hygiene rules affect all aspects of the food chain that links producers to consumers. At Mimi's butcher ship in Altamura, meeting food safety protocols is obvious as soon as you enter his small shop. The sleek, modern, refrigerated cases would be familiar to any North American customer except

The yellow tag in the goat's ear helps a health inspector track the animal's health on his regular visits.

for one thing: they are all empty. The Hygiene Package requires that food storage locations be designed to allow for optimal temperature which can be monitored and recorded. This sounds quite sensible--except that Mimi's customers don't shop that way. They don't browse. Customers who come in have a long-standing relationship with Mimi; they know exactly what he carries and what they want, and Mimi cuts it for them while they visit. If anything, the cases are used for standing orders, or phone orders that are waiting for a quick pick up (or for chilling wine!).

Mimi is a third-generation butcher, and learned butchery when butchers also slaughtered animals. His meat is sourced from no more than fifty kilometers away, with sheep coming from even closer. He knows the farmers and shepherds, and has done for decades. He knows how the animals have been treated, how healthy they are, what they have been fed, and how they were slaughtered. This gives him the confidence to try the raw pork as he makes sausages, and when he offers me some, I trust him enough to accept. As I ate raw pork, and contemplated the horrified responses of many of the North Americans present, I concluded that to eat meat raw you must know where the meat is coming from and have a trust that the animal was healthy and butchered properly. When these connections are lost in the gigantic scale of the industrial food system, there is nothing for the consumer to build trust from save the certifications, inspections, and legislated regulations. And so the vicious circle continues. These policies are important in the context of large industrial facilities; I wouldn't eat raw pork from a giant meat-packing plant or a faceless grocery store. But they are really blunt instruments designed to address food safety concerns from the large-scale, industrial, food system.

A one-size-fits-all approach doesn't work well for products made by human hands. Accumulated knowledge passed down through generations of producers has distilled the magic of microbes in the transformation of milk into cheese, with the subtle variations that come with the type of cheese made, the milk used, and whether it is raw or pasteurized. Many are calling for small producers to be exempt from the Hygiene Package, or to have the exemptions more clearly defined and communicated. The Slow Food Movement is an important voice of advocacy, and is helping small food producers navigate these complex and expensive rules so that food diversity can be protected while also addressing the welfare of consumers. It's a hard balance to strike.

Living tradition

Part of defining tradition as a dynamic co-production means keeping it alive and relevant in new contexts. This is at the heart of the Messors philosophy, and you can understand the fundamentals of this when you visit Jesce, where it all began for Tonio over two decades ago. My first visit to this site was on the morning of my departure back to Canada. On only a handful of hours of sleep, we assembled a simple picnic breakfast and cast out across the rolling wheat fields past Tonio's family olive grove and summer home to Jesce, an archaeological site dating to the Neolithic. Tonio spent fourteen years working on restoring walls, the cave entrance, and stunning rupestral church frescos (dating from the 1300s), but could never secure a contract from the municipality. Ultimately, the contract, and attached funding, was given to an architectural company with a very different vision for restoration; they built walls not in keeping with the original style or design, low walls that cut across the courtyard where people would have communally worked their grains and woven their sheep's wool. Perhaps the most tragic element of the story though is that with all of this investment of energy and money, the site is now all but abandoned, used periodically by the poet Donato Emar Laborante for artistic performances. Carefully restored walls are again beginning to tumble down. The neglect highlights a critical disconnect in archaeology and heritage management: why put the work in if the site isn't maintained? Why is this heritage important, relevant, and worth the investment?

Donato stands in the entrance to Jesce's cave church, the colourful frescos lit by the sunlight outside.

Experiences at Jesce seem to have crystalized the Messors philosophy, whereby preservation is defined in a dynamic way that embraces the reuse and reimagining of space that has been happening in places like this for centuries. In contrast to the ethic of a "pristine" heritage site that appears to dominate the conservation philosophy of North America, sites are being revalued in a modern context. At Jesce, Tonio reconstructed key elements of the site but also built a stage and concrete floor in the cave for year round performances, breathing new life and relevance into a site that has been important for various reasons for thousands of years. Fornello will be the same: ancient caves, used at various times by both shepherds and Byzantine monks escaping the persecution of the Balkans, and the limestone shepherd's house that has been abandoned for at least 150 years become the locus for art restoration, participatory tourism, cheese-making and sustainable rural economic development. Tradition is not an artifact of "yesteryear"; it is in a continuous state of invention in the present. It is dynamic, a shape shifter that is constantly being produced and reproduced to suit the needs of context. As circumstances dictate tradition's many forms, the hope is that it maintains its relevance to all who co-produce it in an ever-changing world.

18. Bread

Altamura bread is one of Italy's most famous breads, and has been recognized with the European Union's DOP (*Denominazione di Origine Protetta*) status, which protects its name, origin, and specifics of production. Like so many of the food traditions of southern Italy, this bread is a product whose origin is deeply rooted in the ancient peasant traditions of the Alta Murgia. The lactic acid that is created in the fermentation process creates a film that keeps the crumb moist for about ten days, which is part of the magic of Altamura bread. This unique ability to preserve the taste and softness for a relatively long time made it an excellent food for shepherds to take with them as they walk the more rural parts of Puglia, returning to town every two weeks with their dairy products. The bread is so tasty that it has been memorialized in one of Horace's poems: while the water of Altamura was not considered very good, "... *their bread is exceeding fine, inasmuch that the weary traveler is used to carry it willingly on his shoulders.*"

People in Puglia eat a lot of bread. It is a staple with every meal and it is really inexpensive (one kilogram generally costs 1 to 1.5 euros). Not surprisingly, there is a huge demand for wheat and bread. The rolling countryside is blanketed by fields of golden durum wheat in June, but wheat has been a key import commodity since Roman times. People did not begin baking bread at home until after World War II when households started to buy modern ovens as kitchen appliances. Prior to this time it was difficult to get an oven hot enough to bake bread, and it was an uncomfortable prospect at the height of summer; for these reasons, the job of baking bread fell to a specialist (the *fornaio*) who ran a communal bread oven. It was much more fuel efficient this way too. Ovens like the ones at Il Forno Antico di Santa Caterina date to the 1400s (although the building around it was constructed in 1724). Historically, there were more than fifty such ovens in Altamura, a high number given the size of the town. Families had set days and times to bring their dough to the ovens to be baked. A person would pick up and deliver the dough to the bakery via a three to four meter plank balanced on his shoulder. The dough was carefully placed along the board to remember who it belonged to, and the loaves would be branded just before going into the oven to keep track of individual loaves amongst the several hundred baked at a time. Once baked, the loaves would be delivered back to the proper families, and in keeping with the use of food in this informal economy, the delivery boy would be paid with a portion of bread. People paid the baker with dough, which he either used to feed his own family, sold, or used to satisfy his contract with the church.

Today, as few people bake their own bread at home, there is no need for delivery boys or brands, and these bakeries are once again communal in a sense; the only difference is that the neighbourhood's bread is made there from start to finish.

The concept of communal ovens dwindled after World War II and ended altogether in Altamura in the 1980s when most people stopped making their own bread and started to buy it instead. The business of the *fornaio* changed from baking bread to making it. Pino, the baker at the Forno Antico di Santa Catarina, usually starts the dough around 2:00 am so that there is fresh bread coming out of the oven to sell to customers who come in before work. The rhythm of the baker is dictated by elements that are often out of his control. Every day is a dance between the baker and the dough; some days the dough takes longer to knead or rise because of the temperature. Part of the DOP designation requires precise quantities of the very few ingredients that build Altamura bread: every 100kg of dough requires 60L of water, 2 kg of salt, and 20kg of sourdough starter. The water is generally 18 degrees Celsius, but slight adjustments are made based on the weather. Historically the bread was reportedly kneaded for twenty minutes by hand, which may be the secret to its almost magical longevity--and what made it so attractive to travelers and shepherds. Lengthy kneading by hand is not possible when a single bakery is producing over two hundred loaves a day from scratch, so today the dough is mixed in a machine with a specially designed pair of hooks that mimic a woman's hands and arms mixing and kneading the ingredients together.

The dough rises until its first shaping, starting around 5:00 am. Traditionally, the loaves were bigger than today, as much as five or six kilograms each. These huge loaves worked well for shepherds who would take them out to pastures for up to two weeks. Today, loaves are made in half and one kilogram sizes. Portions of dough are weighed out and deftly shaped into rounds; the dough is soft and light and the air smells of yeast and wood smoke. After the first shaping, the dough rests for 45 minutes before the second round of shaping begins. The loaves are made in two traditional forms: a low, rounded loaf, *"a cappidde de prèvete"*(priest's hat), and a tall loaf that is folded over on itself called *"U sckuanète"* (meaning "folded loaf" in the local dialect). The final shaping is done just before the loaf is put into the oven; for the folded loaf, the dough is quickly rolled into a short log and then the forearm is used to flatten the dough half way along the log. The two ends are then stacked on top of each other, the dough is popped on a long-handled peel, and then loaded into the cavernous, domed oven. Oven temperature is kept at 260-280 degrees Celsius (500-540 F) until the fire is banked and the door is closed.

The loaves rest for about 45 minutes and then cook for 75 minutes with the oven door closed, but for many of the first loaves the "rest" time is actually inside the oven. It takes 45 minutes to fill the oven with the 250 loaves that are baked daily before the fire is banked and the door is closed for about an hour, so loaves that are put in first, at the back edges of the oven, cook for much longer than the ones put in last. The result is a variety of loaves ranging from very well done, with a dark brown crust, to less well

Smoke curls above the loaves of bread and focaccia in the cavernous oven. The focaccia is pulled out just before the door is closed, sealing in the heat for over an hour of baking.

done, with a golden brown crust, variations to satisfy every customer. In a nod to meeting modern consumer trends, the bakery has recently started baking a decidedly non-DOP loaf using three ancient grains (spelt, einkorn, and emmer). As always, producers must respond to market interests to maintain their relevance in their communities. There is also an impressive array of gluten-free products in Altamura, which in the land of gluten is quite a feat.

While some ovens bake bread several times a day, Pino bakes bread only once a day. His business is now open seven days a week to supply the increased demand for bread due to local tourism. He sells almost every loaf he makes daily.

Pane di Altamura
(Altamura Bread)

There is no specific Altamura bread recipe for home baking to be found. Based on DOP requirements for ingredients and cooking conditions--not the least of which is context--Altamura bread can *only* be made in one place. However, these hints, combined with the approximate times and temperatures discussed at the Santa Catarina bakery make it possible to create a passable version to enjoy at home. Would Horace approve?

1kg (7-8 cups) durum wheat (remilled semolina)
200g natural yeast
20g (2.5 Tbsps) sea salt
600 ml (~1 ¼ cups) warm water

Make a well in the centre of the flour and add the other ingredients. Work the ingredients together until the dough is smooth and uniform. Pino at the Santa Catarina bakery kneads his bread for *much* longer than most home bakers. (Dough for 80 loaves is mixed and kneaded for 40 minutes in the mechanical mixer.)

Cover with a tea towel and leave for about 2 hours. Knead again, shaping the dough into a tight round loaf. Let rest for 2 hours or more at room temperature to rise a second time. The dough should rise about 1.5 times its original volume.

Preheat the oven to 480 F. Invert the dough onto a floured surface, score a cross on top (for a low round loaf) or shape into a folded loaf, and bake in a hot oven for 20 minutes. Lower the temperature gradually to 350 F degrees and bake for a further 45-50 minutes (60-70 minutes overall). If you have a baking stone or tiles, use them!

A Shepherd's Lunch

Bread was a critical daily component of the shepherd's diet in Puglia, and still is. Nothing is wasted, so hard bread over a week old was transformed into *cialda calda*--bread soup--to keep it palatable. Another version, *cialda fredda*, or bread salad, is a beautiful complement to this simple but delicious meal.

Cialda calda
(Bread Soup)

Make a simple stock with salted water. Throw in whole garlic cloves, sliced celery and onion, parsley, diced potatoes, and tomatoes. Once this has simmered for long enough to cook the potatoes, poach some eggs in the stock. Ladle this mixture over sliced bread that has been layered in the bottom of a serving bowl.

Cialda fredda
(Bread Salad)

Tear bread into chunks and place in a bowl. Cut up cucumbers, red onion, garlic, tomatoes, radishes, and black olives and add on top. Dress the salad with a liberal dose of extra virgin olive oil, salt, fresh fennel and thyme, and lemon juice.

19. Slow Food in a Fast World

Taste, like identity, has value only when there are differences.
-Carlo Petrini

McDonald's is a symbol of modernity and globalization; the traveler can be comforted that a McDonald's will offer familiar food in unfamiliar places, a homogenization that really seems to sum up the industrial food system. The success of McDonald's has been based on standardization and efficiency, watchwords of the fast-paced industrial world. In 2001, the Golden Arches came to Altamura. The restaurant was centrally located just outside the historic district, its neon-lit sign casting a glow on the shiny limestone streets at all hours of the day. The local food association saw the arrival of McDonald's as an invasion, clear evidence of changes that had been creeping into the city for several decades. It later characterized the community response as a war, with focaccia and Altamura bread being used as bullets. But when you talk to people who were living there at the time, what shines through is indifference; after some initial curiosity, Altamurans went back to eating focaccia bread, which could be conveniently purchased right next to McDonald's for just over a euro. Not only was a chunk of focaccia much cheaper than a McDonald's hamburger, the success of multiple bakeries in the city has rested on each bakery producing a focaccia bread with a unique taste, which in turn creates their own regular, loyal customers. Celebrating the global brand, and the standard, homogenized flavour that represents the industrial food system, was a tactical error on McDonald's part; the corporate giant didn't recognize that despite having a population of 75,000, Altamura still thinks like a small town that likes its local food. The franchise closed in December 2002, after being open less than two years, and the French publication *Libération* described the windows of the restaurant being covered *"like a shroud on the victim of a culinary battlefield."* In retrospect, this has been hailed as a significant moment in the explicit appreciation of local food traditions.

The friction between McDonald's, an emblem of the broader industrial food reality, and small-scale local food traditions is not isolated to Altamura. The story of the Slow Food Movement starts with a McDonald's restaurant that opened near the iconic Spanish Steps in Rome in 1986, but Slow Food is a response to changes that really started to accelerate after the Second World War. Carlo Petrini, the founder of the Slow Food movement, saw McDonald's as more than a fast-food outlet. It represented the relentless march of modernity, often associated with Americanization, which he and others felt was robbing Italy of its unique identity. That the restaurant opened in Rome's iconic historic district just added insult to injury. Italy's "Economic Miracle" (the name for the country's embrace of industrialism and modernity beginning in the 1950s) was meant to transform the poor nation into a European, industrial power. Changes were profound and varied, but the shift from share cropper farmers to factory workers led to a cascade effect that was epitomized by the arrival of McDonald's in Rome, the straw breaking the camel's back in a way. It is estimated that between 1951 and 1971 nine million people left the rural landscapes of Italy for large urban centres, particularly those in the north. On the agricultural side this was facilitated by new technologies like tractors and herbicides that made much of the human labour of the farm redundant. Additionally, small, family farms had a hard time competing, leading to sales and amalgamation of ever bigger farms. The movement of such large numbers of people profoundly affected community and family structures, personal economics, and diet. The modern consumer economy suddenly presented itself, and more of the population had money to spend in it. The trappings of this modern reality could be seen in more cars on roads, the appearance of refrigerators in kitchens, and a diet that incorporated more and more meat, an expression of newfound socio-economic opportunity. According to the research done by John Dicke, in 1861 average annual meat consumption nationally was only 12 kilograms (about 26.5 lbs) per person (or 33 grams per day, which amounts to about half the weight of an egg). The amount had doubled by 1960, which is interesting to think about in the context of the Mediterranean diet, defined by Ancel Keys in the 1950s at the cusp of these great food changes. By 1975, the average Italian was consuming 170 grams of meat per day, a far cry from the near-vegetarian diet touted as the cornerstone of Mediterranean tradition and wellbeing.

By the 1980s it was becoming obvious that the economic boom was jeopardizing the culinary heritage of rural Italy. Petrini noticed, with alarm, that a growing number of people no longer had direct connections with their food. Not only were people no longer producing their own food, but increasingly they were not buying it directly from food producers, preferring instead the convenience of modern one-stop grocery stores. People didn't know the baker who got up hours before dawn to bake fresh bread, or the butcher who had a lifelong relationship with the farmer who provided him with the meat that he cured for *charcuterie* or stuffed into sausage casings. They didn't know the man who tended the sheep and transformed the milk into cheese. Perhaps Petrini met a youth, like I did, who lived surrounded by olive trees yet thought that olive oil came from pressing the pit. This disconnect threatened to accelerate the decay of traditional foodways, without consumers even really noticing.

The protest against the arrival of McDonald's in historic Rome galvanized something of a food revolution. The Slow Food Movement's manifesto clearly states its mission: *Against the universal madness of the Fast Life, we need to choose the defense of tranquil material pleasure. Against those, and there are many of them, who confuse efficiency with frenzy, we propose the vaccine of a sufficient portion of assured sensual pleasure, to be practiced in slow and prolonged enjoyment.* Since food is central to life, the kitchen seems like a good place to start the protest against the high-velocity, industrial reality. Slow Food's mandate is summarized in three integrated pillars: food should be Good, Clean, and Fair.

Key to Slow Food's definition of "Good" food is the rediscovery of flavour and the enjoyment of eating. Instead of eating to live, the Slow Food Manifesto advocates living to eat, where a focus on quality over quantity produces an awareness of the flavours of regional cooking and the knowledge of small food producers. Enjoying food, instead of just fueling the body, is to be actively sought and celebrated. "Clean" food speaks to the importance of environmental sustainability, and the holistic relationship between food, humans, and landscapes. The choices we make in terms of what we eat have major effects on the environment and society. When we choose to buy cheese from a local shepherd, we are not only getting "Good" food, but a product that supports local biodiversity represented in the shepherd's pasture that is threatened by the march of large-scale, mono-cropped wheat agriculture. Preserving and sustainably promoting small producers supports cultural *and* biological diversity in this complex dance that weaves together the natural landscape and the human one. As Carlo Petrini said, "*Any gastronome who is not an environmentalist is stupid, and any environmentalist who is not a gastronome is sad.*"

The third pillar, "Fair" food, means different things for consumers and producers, and is perhaps the trickiest of the three. Food produced in small quantities by artisan producers generally costs more than mass-produced food. This can price it out of reach for many consumers. Fair food for consumers then is good, clean, *and* accessible. But this is hard to deliver. Without economy of scale, producers have to charge more to make a living wage, but can have a very hard time competing in the global market. The state of lemon farmers on the Amalfi Coast is a case in point: when you can buy imported lemons for a third of the price of Amalfi lemons, the writing is on the wall for Amalfi lemon producers--unless consumers make choices based on quality. To be fair to producers, there has to be fair compensation, otherwise farmers will abandon the labour intensive food production that runs generations deep in their families and communities, or migrant labour will be exploited to minimize the overhead. The Slow Food Movement has been outspoken about deplorable work conditions and the use of vulnerable immigrant workers--cheap tomato sauce from the fields of Puglia may be accessible to consumers but is far from fair for pickers. Finding a way to deliver food that is fair to everyone at the table is where Slow Food becomes a political advocacy organization. It is only when state subsidies support and promote small-scale food producers, the keepers of generations of food traditions shaped by the landscape and in turn shaping both the landscape and the humans that call it home, that fairness can be realized. Slow Food combines politics, history, philosophy and anthropology; the result is a resistance movement whose message has extended well beyond Rome and Italy. Slow Food is now represented in over 150 countries worldwide; the challenges and degradation that Petrini was responding to in the 1980s is not isolated to the Italian peninsula.

The voice of Slow Food is essential in the din of globalization and homogenization, but what does the concept actually mean? How do you embody a slow food philosophy? Maybe it starts with the reminder that the Greek intention behind the word "diet" (*dieta*) is about lifestyle, not just food. Although the name is meant to be in opposition to the fast food likes of McDonald's, much of the concept of Slow Food comes down to pace, or what geographer Robert Levine calls tempo. The standardization and efficiency of the industrial food system, of which McDonald's is a part, are elements of a fast-food culture regardless of whether you eat at fast-food restaurants. The pace of industrialized modernity is near frantic. The average time that Americans spend commuting on any given work day is just over fifty minutes (although some spend considerably longer). Add the expectation of an 8.5 hour work day, children's soccer practices and music lessons, and the reality that the vast majority of households do not have a stay-at-home parent to prepare meals, and you start to understand how food becomes an unfortunate casualty in this context, deprioritized in terms of procurement yet still essential for us biologically. So we outsource the production of nearly everything, from bread and pasta to tomato sauce, and are happy to have someone else (some faceless person in some unknown place) process and prepare our food so that we can feed ourselves and our families amid the demands of our very busy lives. When tempo hits a fever pitch, food can become fuel, the ultimate disconnect since humans are not machines.

Part of Slow Food is literally the advice to slow down, to explicitly enjoy acquiring ingredients, preparing a meal, and consuming it, preferably in the company of others (a recent report found that over fifty percent of food consumption in the US happens when the consumer is alone!). According to Petrini, "[b]eing Slow means that you control the rhythms of your own life. What we are *fighting for is the right to determine our own tempos.*" Supporting the producers of distinctive local products turns everyone into co-producers (Slow Food's favoured term for consumers), with vested interests in maintaining these products. Although modernity has brought a lot of changes to southern Italy, the tempo of slow food culture is still expressed in everyday activities of life in Altamura. You can witness it as groups of men stroll the shiny limestone streets of town in the evening, in laundry hung out to dry instead of being thrown into an energy-hungry dryer. Food is fresh, seasonal, and local, and purchased almost daily, very different from North Americans shopping for the week, which means that food is not as fresh, requires additives to prolong shelf life, and just doesn't taste as good! When you eat mostly fresh food and shop daily there is less concern about spoilage in a cool pantry, nor is there the need to compromise the flavour of things like cucumbers or tomatoes by putting them in the fridge so that they will last all week. This lifestyle is reflected in unexpected ways, like the size of one's fridge. Whereas the typical North American fridge has increased in size quite significantly in the last fifty years to accommodate the efficiency of shopping only once a week, the fridges in Altamura are small and bare by my standards. At the *masseria* eggs are kept out, most cheeses are kept out (part of their natural aging), and leftovers are covered with a plate or a tea towel to deter flies. The only items that earn fridge space are raw meats, ricotta and other fresh cheeses, milk, and white wine!

Critiques of the Slow Food Movement

I think the merits of the Slow Food Movement's philosophy are clear; it's when you start trying to apply the philosophy to the real world that you start to see some problems. It starts with the fact that celebrating food that is good, clean, and fair generally means paying more for it; but realistically this is not financially possible for a lot of people. Slow Food has been charged with being elitist, and this extends beyond issues of accessibility. Slow Food suffers from the impression that one must acquire a "taste" and knowledge about a product to truly "consume with pleasure." Explicitly embracing pleasure can be interpreted as a form of decadence only possible for the elite that have the time and money to enjoy good food. Slow foods, which can be consumed at leisure, can reflect the superior taste of the consumer. This cultivation of connoisseurship smacks of aristocracy and exclusivity, and seems inappropriate to apply to good "peasant food." Creating more accessible opportunities to consume with pleasure is possible through awareness, the explicit appreciation of the effort, knowledge and meaning represented in real food. Growing even a small amount of your own food makes you appreciate the efforts of farmers. Meeting butchers and cheese makers lets you appreciate the knowledge that is required to conjure the foods we enjoy. Spending forty-five minutes cleaning mussels before cooking them and shelling them for a pasta sauce reminds you of the amount of preparation that goes into a meal where fresh food is served rather than opening a can of shellfish. This appreciation is not demonstrated by one's ability to discuss the nose and complex finish of an expensive wine, but rather, very simply, if it tastes good, *this* becomes the only certification that is required.

Europe's move to highlight and support quality products is a good fit with Italy's diverse and specialized agriculture, and the aims of the Slow Food Movement. The risk, though, is that peasant food may be transformed into something "artisan" or "traditional" by way of a DOP stamp that is then only accessible to more affluent consumers. This can make our evaluation of terms like "traditional" and "authentic" quite confusing. Altamura bread is a great example of this: bread that is DOP-certified costs more. The baker pays more for the local durum wheat and the certification itself costs money, so DOP bread is about twice as expensive as non-certified loaves (2.5 to 3 euros per kilogram). This may not be financially sustainable in a place where people expect cheap bread (1 to 1.5 euros per kilogram is common for a non-certified loaf) and eat it with every meal.

Another interesting tension is that the focus of Slow Food (and the Mediterranean diet) is generally rustic, peasant food traditions, called *la cucina povera* in much of Italy. It is somewhat ironic that the modern affluent eater is connecting with the foodways historically consumed by fairly poor peasants, foods that the elite of the time, the ones living in the comfort of the *masserie* or in cities did not eat, or even avoided because they had other options. It is easy to forget that peasants generally lived in the shadow of hunger; the poverty-driven, near vegetarianism is now a venerated foundation of the Mediterranean diet. The local food focus of the Slow Food movement was a reality for most Italians because of circumstance (i.e., poverty) rather than out of some expression of morality: they ate what they had.

In promoting food heritage, particularly for an outside audience, we also have to be careful not to create fantasies that project contemporary meanings onto the past. There are many foods that are celebrated today as elements of the Mediterranean diet or Italian identity that meant very different things in the past. Chestnuts are a good example: while a fall festival in the Mugello region between Florence and Bologna dedicated to sweet chestnuts sounds like an excellent expression of Slow Food, one should keep in mind that until recently chestnuts were the "bread of the poor" and not considered a sign of happy times but rather of misery and hunger. However, it is clear that in places like Matera, *la cucina povera* is a new source of pride and identity. Part of its appeal may be the contrast with a modern, industrialized reality, a yearning to return to a romanticized past. Local food can become a counterpoint to the homogenizing tendencies of modernity, something that can be hyper-unique for towns and regions and thus useful in making the distinctions that are important both for local identity but also the cultural capital that draws tourists. What is nice to see is that Materans are cooking local dishes for themselves again in their own kitchens, so the renewed interest in local foods is rewarding to more than just tourists.

Slow Food recognizes that foodways are not static museum artifacts. But it is difficult to celebrate dynamic food traditions in a modern world. Protection can be constraining; Slow Food has a hard time incorporating fusion food and ethnic influence. Today's world of global influence (especially with Italy's history of tomatoes from America and pasta from the Arabs) has created a polychromatic cuisine that reflects these complex realities, both ancient and contemporary. In this way Slow Food appears to be quite conservative, with narrow definitions of tradition and authenticity that in some sense stagnate culture. Italian foodways are just as susceptible to the erosion of diversity and cultural meaning at the hands of industrial society as any. The Italian diet clearly reflects the fast-paced transformations of the last century. Yet Italy nurtures a food conservatism that cherishes culinary values and upholds these elements of identity despite the powerful influences of globalization (or tries to maintain both). North American cuisine as a whole has embraced the expression of ethnic diversity and the colonial history of immigration. In sporting a food culture that lacks the deep heritage roots of homelands, it is more flexible and (except for regional and ethnic examples) more easily accommodates a disconnect with food. In contrast, Italy appears more reluctant to make these compromises and sacrifices. Slow Food and DOP certification (both relatively new) are emblems of this reluctance.

In his treatise *Democracy in America*, nineteenth-century philosopher Alexis de Tocqueville argues that much of the character of the American psyche can be traced to the founding population of immigrants. The bravery and desperation that made so many poor immigrants get on boats and sail into the unknown selected for a population of fearless idealists always searching for something better and having nothing to lose. The momentum of the settling of the American West may be a good historical example of this, but I wonder if a similar argument can be made in terms of the relationship between American immigrant populations and food. The food that many left behind was horrendous poverty food, and a fresh start in America meant casting off the yoke of much of this food with such sorrowful memories. Immigrant populations are also a mash up of different regions and traditions that take on a new blended identity: what would be considered Cantonese food in China becomes Chinese food in North America, and the regional differences of Italian foodways merge into contemporary expressions of Italian-American cuisine. So maybe due to historical circumstances, and an overall, youth-dominant, North American culture, we see very different connections to and consumption of food--an adventurous, flexible fusion rather than food conservatism. This is not to say that this conservatism isn't appealing to North Americans; it is a clear draw for tourists and a growing trend in North American community identity building. Italian food conservatism encourages food nostalgia, whereby "genuine" artisan food is contrasted with industrial food. Food considered typical, authentic, and traditional is embraced, without much reflection on how these vague terms are defined (by whom, and for what purpose).

Despite the critique, Slow Food has something incredibly important to offer. The movement encourages putting a face to a food, celebrating the connection between products and the people and landscapes that have produced them. In focusing on an "artisanal" style instead of "industrial" production, Slow Food is emphasizing the importance of the social life of foods, which ultimately contributes to their high quality, and unique flavours. Operationally, the movement is as important politically and economically as it is culturally, using its resources and voice to support the passion of small food producers. Local Slow Food chapters, called "*convivia*," are generally spearheaded not by the producers themselves but the urban consumers who want to protect and promote local foodways. These local Slow Food chapters connect the producers with the movement, which can then lend support by helping to navigate the confusing landscape of bureaucracy to secure exemptions from EU hygiene regulations, or find loans and grants. Slow Food also offers publicity resources to find markets for products, both locally and internationally. In offering support, these non-food producers have an opportunity to reconnect with the land and the foods from these landscapes, and truly become "co-producers" rather than just consumers. This really speaks to a key element of the movement: engagement. Becoming aware of what it takes to produce good food--knowledge, dedication, sacrifice, pride, relationships, time--and then actively supporting this by purchasing, makes you part of the production of that food.

An interesting thing happens when you start to appreciate and promote food traditions. Some have argued that the inhabitants of southern Italy have historically taken their local food for granted, and the arrival of modernity in the shape of McDonald's "Golden Arches" was the wake up call to save these expressions of heritage, identity and place through explicit effort. The process of getting DOP designation for Altamura bread, or getting the delicious cherry- and almond-filled cookies from Ceglie Messapica certified as a Slow Food artisanal product are new forms of appreciation, but are not the only ways to bring the philosophy of slow food into one's life. The criticisms of Slow Food's elitism are fair; socio-economics certainly make the enjoyment of high-quality food more obtainable for some than others. A more realistic approach is to make changes in areas of our lives where there is more direct control, often with little added expense. Choosing to use fresh ingredients has the cascade effect of supporting local producers and the continuation of that knowledge in your community, but it is not a selfless act. Making meals that are delicious, nutritious, and not full of additives can be a source of personal pride as, oven mitts in hand, one brings a simple frittata to the dinner table.

Concluding thoughts

As an anthropologist I am interested in the connections between seemingly disparate subjects. Talking about food can open conversations about biology, environment, history, philosophy, even religion. The chapters of this book have presented a number of repeated themes, whether discussing olive oil, or shepherds, or nuns and pastries. Most of these traditions developed in response to a landscape that has not changed all that much in centuries but exist today in a social reality that has changed dramatically in just a few generations. Paramount has been the connection between humans and the landscape: low intensity agriculture and pastoralism woven together to make the most of rocky, dry environments, and sustainability practices to manage the precious water resource to get what one needs but rarely more. These traditions seem out of sync with a modern world that focuses on individual competition and monetary success, won through short-term unsustainable use of landscapes that are bent to the will of humans. The food traditions of southern Italy were forged in a context where communal food production was a mainstay of the region's social organization and informal economy. Families and neighbours helped one another, and were encouraged to do so out of a deep sense of moral obligation: it was just what you *did!* This is in contrast to industrialized North America, which is built on the characteristics of individualism and upward mobility (amongst others), where people are encouraged to value independence and personal advancement over communal prosperity. Indeed, this has become the backbone of capitalism. These differences may in part be due to geography: group members in North America are scattered to better access personal opportunities like school and work, and invest personal effort in individual success rather than communal effort for shared benefits. This has heightened the labour specialization that is now required in North American society: only two percent of North Americans are farmers, supporting a complex assortment of specialists who, as consumers, can be quite geographically and psychologically disconnected from their food and members of their community. It is no surprise that part of the Myth of Tuscany that is so compelling to tourists is the idea of being more connected to community and food production. The fast-paced lifestyle that is selected for and then required to support a fiercely independent consumer culture can feel impersonal and out of touch with life's most basic elements: food, family, community, and landscape.

What is important to recognize, though, is that the same things are happening in rural Italy. Since World War II there has been an exodus of people from the south, drawn to the factory work of large cities in the north, or the promise of a better life through emigration. Ongoing unemployment in places like Altamura fuels these ongoing relocations. When communities are fractured by family members moving away, it is difficult to find people with the moral obligation to participate in food production work in a reciprocal way. Workers must be hired to harvest the olives and the grapes that are made into olive oil and wine, which can make maintaining small family groves and vineyards prohibitively expensive. Or cheap labour like the tomato industry becomes the solution that offers financial benefit to a few, and vulnerability and insecurity to many. Many small farmers are selling out, and larger corporate producers move in. Sometimes producers simply abandon groves and gardens rather than working exceptionally hard to harvest products that will lose money in a competitive global economy awash in fake olive oil and cheap imported lemons.

Although the words inheritance and heritage are used in different contexts in English, they share a common Latin root--*hereditare*, meaning "condition or state transmitted from ancestors." *Inheritance* usually means the passing down of tangible assets, such as land or money from generation to generation. In contrast, the word *heritage* is used to reference traditions and elements of the past (such as archaeological sites), often less tangible but equally important cultural capital. This cultural capital is under threat from many angles; it is often at odds with modern development that has different priorities and can tap global markets to find cheaper ways to make and consume items. I'm not sure that these traditions can survive when the measure of value is based solely on supply and demand, and when there is a narrow emphasis on profit. When the focus is only on end products, the intricate relationships between the parts of a cultural system are easily missed. Amalfi lemons offer a very clear example: the human labour involved in farming these challenging environments makes it impossible for farmers to complete when it comes to price. That cheap, imported lemons are inferior quality is immaterial at a certain point; faced with such a huge difference in price we can guess what type of lemons most Italians are purchasing. It is also not surprising that given these realities farms are being abandoned, and younger generations are not following in their parents' footsteps. But just like the cascade of changes that occur when an ecosystem loses a key, contributing species, when the gardens are abandoned the terraces quickly degrade, and without upkeep they no longer stabilize the steep slopes above towns along the ocean that are tourist meccas. And as climate change brings increased rain and more intense storms to the region, the threat of landslides increases; now the value of Amalfi lemons is harder to quantify.

Heritage also implies succession and legacy, but for heritage to be inherited it must be maintained. This does not mean it has to be preserved in a frozen, unchanging form; when you think about inheriting your parents' house you realize it isn't the same as when they bought it. The whims of owners lead to additions, new windows, a different paint job, all of which reflect contemporary needs and realities. This is tricky to think about when it comes to heritage, in great part because of the Western definition of preservation brought to us by museums. Like that fancy china in our grandmother's buffet, which was never used for fear of something getting broken, we expect to preserve things in pristine condition or they lose their value. Items are carefully conserved as a snapshot of an artifact or site's history and put behind glass in a state of arrested development. Theoretically they should look exactly the same forever, a heritage legacy for future generations. But where is the fun to be had with the pristine period Barbie doll that is still in its original packaging? It is a collector's item to be sure, but only really worth something in monetary terms, and only when it is sold. I don't think you can put a price on the enjoyment of childhood play and the memories that come from playing with a toy, even though that use leaves its mark (or a missing limb!). The same applies to food heritage; it must remain a living, breathing entity, able to absorb and reflect the influences of time and space. This is muted when modernity is defined as only looking ahead, or tradition is defined in contrast to it, creating a stark choice between the two.

Also related is the word "heir"; nothing can be inherited if there is no one to accept it. When the shepherd is valued and there is more demand for his product, more youth will become shepherds and be able to stay in the communities that have been the basis for their family geography for generations. When the shepherd demographic shifts to include more local young artisans, the interconnected knowledge of animals, landscape, and food is maintained as a living entity rather than a dusty relic in constant need of rescue. Thinking about the total package should go a long way towards re-establishing the sustainability that has been the secret to the success of humans in the southern Italian peninsula for thousands of years.

Looking more broadly, one sees the value of these traditions in a more complex way. But since changing the capitalist system seems improbable in the short term, it falls to individuals to value the intangible elements of these food traditions and the people who perpetuate them. Not only do these foods often taste much better than their mass-produced counterparts, the stories that are represented, and the process of engaging with food producers and the landscapes they occupy, feed something deep within us, which is immensely satisfying. Food-based tourism clearly has a contribution to make here in terms of generating another form of value, but this will need to be developed carefully and with explicit recognition of the power of the Tourist Gaze to shape and co-opt. There is a real danger in casting tourism enterprises as the heroic saviours because it marginalizes the role of local food producers in the process, and can be quite patronizing. The shepherd does not ask for salvation, but rather, needs support to redefine his craft in a modern world. Support rather than salvation is a crucial distinction.

A tourist in rural Italy can contribute to sustainable economic development and be rewarded with memorable, authentic opportunities to interact with real food producers making exceptional food, food that is not only good to eat, but in the words of Claude Levi-Strauss *"good to think."* Of equal value is an appreciation for the modern challenges of maintaining traditions that are considered so novel and appealing to visitors seeking them as part of the tourist experience. These opportunities may seem more attainable while on vacation, but small food producers and their passion, knowledge, and determination to maintain their lifeways are everywhere. The industrial food system seems to be defined by homogenized anonymity, where food loses its connection with people, place, season, and symbolism. Vibrant, local food cultures are fiercely staking a claim to tourists' local geographies in North America and Britain. Their stories are just as important as the ones presented here, and the lasting souvenir of culinary-based tourism is the desire to reconnect with food and its makers in more meaningful ways at home.

References

1. Introduction

Gossling, S.
2003.   Market integration and ecosystem degradation: Is sustainable tourism development in rural communities a contradiction in terms? *Environment, Development and Sustainability* 5(3-4): 383-400.

FAO
1995   Staple Foods; what do people eat? IN: Dimensions of Need: An Atlas of Food and Agriculture. Accessed June 13, 2018 at http://www.fao.org/docrep/u8480e/U8480E07.htm

2. In the *Masseria* Kitchen

Dal Lago Enrico
2005   Agrarian Elites: American Slaveholders and Southern Italian Landowners 1815-1861. Baton Rouge: Louisiana State University Press.

3. Imagining Italy: Culinary tourism and the construction of food identity

Agriturist.
n.d.   *Agriturismo* website. Accessed May 18, 2017: http://www.agriturist.it/en/farm-holidays-italy/1-0.html]

Buckley, R.
2012   Sustainable tourism: Research and reality. *Annals of Tourism Research* 39(2): 528-546.

Bunten, A.
2008   Sharing culture or selling out? Developing the commodified persona in the heritage industry. *American Ethnologist* 35(3): 380-395.

Camera dei Deputati
1998   *Atti parlamentari 4759*. Rome.

Chrzan, J.
n.d.   Dreaming of Tuscany; Pursuing the Anthropology of Culinary
            Tourism. *Expedition*, 49(2): 21-27. Accessed May 3, 2017:
            http://www.penn.museum/documents/publications/expedition/PDFs/49-
            2/Chrzan.pdf

2008   Culinary Tourism: Media Fantasy, Imagined Traditions and
            Transformative Travel. in P. LYSAGHT (ed) *Tourism and Museum:
            Sanitas per Aquas, Spas, Lifestyles and Foodways* : 235-251. Innsbruck:
            Studien Verlay.

Ciervo, M.
2013   Agritourism in Italy and the Local Impact Referring to Itria
            Valley, the Organic Firm "Raggio Verde" and its Ecological
            Agritourism Project. *European Countryside* 4: 322-338.

Cohen, E.
1988   Authenticity and commoditization in tourism. *Annals of Tourism
            Research* 15(3): 371-386.

Cohen, E. and N. Avieli
2004   Food in tourism: Attraction and impediment. *Annals of Tourism
            Research* 31 (4): 755-778.

Dicke, J.
2008   *Delizia! The Epic History of the Italians and Their Food.* New York:
            Simon and Schuster.

Farnesina
n.d.   *The Italian Economy.* Ministero degli Affuri Esteri e della
            Cooperuzione Internazionale. Accessed May 28, 2017:
            http://www.esteri.it/mae/en/ministero/servizi/benvenuti_in_italia/conoscere
            _italia/economia.html

Fodors.
n.d.   Tuscany Travel Guide. Website, accessed May 20, 2017:
            http://www.fodors.com/world/europe/italy/tuscany

Fretchling, D.
1994   Assessing the Impacts of Travel and Tourism- Measuring
            Economic Benefits. In: R. Richie & C. Goeldner (eds) *Travel,
            Tourism and Hospitality Research: A Handbook for Managers and
            Researchers,* 2nd edition:. 359-365. New York: John Wiley & Sons.

Gossling, S and C. Hall
2015   *The Routledge Handbook of Tourism and Sustainability*. London: Routledge.

Gossling, S. and P. Peeters
2015   Assessing tourism's global environmental impact 1900-2050. *Journal of Sustainable Tourism*, 23 (5): 639-659.

Grenoble, R.
2013   Majority of People Consider Quitting Job After a Vacation: Study. *Huffington Post* September 9. Accessed May 3, 2017: http://www.huffingtonpost.com/2013/09/12/vacations-make-us-quit-jobs-monster-study_n_3914979.html

Hertz, C.
2007   The Uniform: As Material, As Symbol, as Negotiated Object. *Midwestern Folklore* 32(1,2): 43-56.

International Culinary Tourism Association (ICTA)
2010   *The State of the Culinary Tourism Industry: Report and Readiness Index*. Portland: International Culinary Tourism Development Publications.

ISTAT
2015   *Italy in Figures*. Rome. Accessed May 26, 2017: http://www.istat.it/en/files/2015/09/ItalyinFigures2015.pdf

Litchfield, R.
1997   The Arab Invasions, and the Medieval Landscape of the "Mediterranean Garden". In E. Seren (ed) *History of the Italian Agricultural Landscape*, 72-73. Princeton: Princeton University Press.

National Geographic
n.d.   National Geographic Expeditions website. Accessed May 21, 2017: www.nationalgeographicexpeditions.com

National Tourism Agency
2012   *Discover Italy: Florence, Tuscany*. Accessed April 20, 2017: http://www.italia.it/en/discoveritaly/tuscany/florence/florence.html?no_cache=1&h=Florence

Lazzeretti, L. and F. Capone
2008   Mapping and Analysing Local Tourism Systems in Italy, 1991–
        2001. *Tourism Geographies* 10 (2): 214-232.

Maccannell, D.
1976   *The Tourist: A New Theory of the Leisure Class*. Berkeley: University
        of California Press.

Mandala Research
2017   The American Culinary Traveler. *Tourism Travel and Research
        Association: Advancing Tourism Research Globally*. 7. Accessed May
        18, 2017:
        http://scholarworks.umass.edu/ttra/2013marketing/White_Papers/7

Mirtaghiyan, M et. al.
2013   A Study of Factors Influencing Food Tourism Branding. *American
        Journal of Tourism Management* 2(3): 63-68.

Mohn, T.
2014   The Rising Wave of Millennial Travelers. Accessed May 20, 2017:
        https://www.forbes.com/sites/tanyamohn/2014/11/08/the-rising-wave-of-
        millennial-travelers/#52290e402bc8

Nestle, M.
1995   Mediterranean diets: historical and research overview. *American
        Journal of Clinical Nutrition* 61: 1313-1320.

O'Connor, A.
2014   Heritage Foodways: Reproducing Identity. *Anthropology News*.

Petrini, C.
2007   *Slow Food Nation: Why Our Food Should Be Good, Clean, and Fair*.
        New York: Rizzoli ex Librus.

Poe, T.
2001   The Labour and Leisure of Food Production as a Mode of Ethnic
        Identity Building Among Italians in Chicago, 1890-1940.
        Rethinking History; The Journal of Theory and Practice Volume 5(1):
        131-148.

Potocnik-Slavic, I. and S. Schmitz
2013   Farm tourism across Europe. *European Countryside* 5(4): 265-274.

Russo, A.
2001   The "vicious circle" of tourism development in heritage cities, *Annals of Tourism Research*, 29(1): 165-182.

Santucci, F.M.
2013   Agritourism for rural development in Italy, evolution, situation and perspectives. *Development*: 16: 186-200.

Sarno, E.
2014   Historical maps and GIS environment as integrated methodology to rediscovery of cattle-track landscapes. a case study. *Review of historical geography and toponomastics* 17-18: 81-101.

Sassoon, D.
1986   *Contemporary Italy: Politics, Economy, and Society since 1945*. New York: Routledge.

Sonninno, R.
2004   For a 'Piece of Bread'? Interpreting Sustainable Development through Agritourism in Southern Tuscany. *Journal of the European Society for Rural Sociology* 44 (3): 285–300.

Stanley, J, and L. Stanley
2015   *Food Tourism: A Practical Marketing Guide*. Oxford: CABI Publications.

Stronza, A.
2001   Anthropology of Tourism: Forging New Ground for Ecotourism and Other Alternatives. *Annual Review of Anthropology* Vol. 30: 261-283.

Travis, D.
n.d.   La Dolce Debbie blog. Accessed May 20, 2017: www.tuscanygetaway.com/BLOG/la-dolce-debbie

UNESCO
n.d.   *The Transhumance: The Royal Shepherd's Track*. Accessed May 1, 2017: http://whc.unesco.org/en/tentativelists/5005/

United Nations
n.d.   UN proclaims 2017 the Year of Sustainable Tourism. Accessed May 10, 2017: http://en.unesco.org/iyst4d

United Nations World Tourism Organization (UNWTO)
2012   *Global Report on Food Tourism, AM Reports Volume 4*. Madrid:
        World Tourism Organization. Accessed May 25 2017
        http://cf.cdn.unwto.org/sites/all/files/docpdf/amreports4-foodtourism.pdf

United Nations World Tourism Organization (UNWTO)
2014   UNWTO World Tourism Barometer. Accessed May 20, 2017:
        http://mkt.unwto.org/barometer.

Urry, J.
2002   *The Tourist Gaze.2nd edition*. London: Sage.

4. Matera

Bernardo, M. and F. De Pascale
2016   Matera A Euro model of Reuse, Sustainability and Resilience.
        Advances in Economics and Business 4(1): 26-36. DOI:
        10.13189/aeb.2016.040104

Dickinson, R.
1954   Land Reform in Southern Italy. *Economic Geography*, Vo. 30, No. 2:
        pp. 157-176. Accessed May 30, 2017: http://www.matera-
        basilicata2019.it/en/mt2019/matera-2019-book.html

European Union (EU)
2014   Selection of the European Capital of Culture Selection Panel's
        Final Report in 2019. Rome. Accessed May 28, 2016: www.matera-
        basilicata2019.it/en

Guida, A. and I. Mecca
2008   The "Palombaro: ("Sassi" of Matera, Italy): The Interaction
        Between Water and Construction Materials. Paper presented at the
        9th International Conference on NDT of Art, Jerusalem Israel, 25-
        30 May 2008. Access June 20, 2018:
        https://www.ndt.net/article/art2008/papers/216Guida.pdf

Toxey, A.
2004   Reinventing the Cave: Competing Images, Interpretations, and
        Representations of Matera, Italy. *Traditional Dwellings and Settlement
        Review* Volume 15(2): pp. 61-78. Accessed June 13, 2018:
        http://iaste.berkeley.edu/pdfs/15.2f-Spr04toxey-sml.pdf

5. Pasta

Dicke, J.
2008   *Delizia! The Epic History of the Italians and Their Food.* New York: Simon and Schuster.

6. Pizza: The taste of poverty in Italy's south

Mattozzi, A. (edited and translated by Zachary Nowak)
2015   Inventing the Pizzeria: A History of Pizza Making in Naples. New York: Bloomsbury.

7. Tomatoes: A "despised and "dangerous" fruit?

Aloisi, S.
2009   "Modern Slave" Migrants Toil in Italy's Tomato Fields. *Reuters.* Accessed May 12, 2017 : http://www.reuters.com/article/us-italy-immigrants-tomatoes-idUSTRE58R1TW20090928

Bir, S.
2014   From Poison to Passion: The Secret History of the Tomato. *Modern Farmer.* Accessed online June 12, 2018: http://modernfarmer.com/2014/09/poison-pleasure-secret-history-tomato/

Davidson, A.
1992   Europeans' Wary Encounter with Tomatoes, Potatoes, and Other New World Foods. In: *Chilies to Chocolate: Food the Americas Gave the World,* edited by Nelson Foster and Linda Cordell, pp. 1-14. Tucson: University of Arizona Press.

Doctors Without Borders
2005   The Fruits of Hypocrisy. Accessed June 12, 2018: http://www.doctorswithoutborders.org/sites/usa/files/MSF-The-Fruits-of-Hypocrisy.pdf

Gentilcore, D.
2010   *Pomodoro! A History of the Tomato in Italy.* New York: Columbia University Press.

Kestryl, Renata
n.d.   Love, Death, or Mere Curisoity? The Tomato in Renaissance Europe. Accessed june 20, 2018: http://www.florilegium.org/?http%3A//www.florilegium.org/files/FOOD-VEGETABLES/Tomatoes-art.html

Mariani, John
2011   *How Italian Food Conquered the World.* Basingstoke: Palgrave Macmillan.

Smith, Annabelle
2013   Why the Tomato Was Feared in Europe for More Than 200 Years. *Smithsonian online* Accessed June 18, 2018:
http://www.smithsonianmag.com/ist/?next=/arts-culture/why-the-tomato-was-feared-in-europe-for-more-than-200-years-863735/

8. Olives and "Liquid Gold"

Angus, Julie
2014   *Olive Odyssey: Searching for the Secrets of the Fruit That Seduced the World.* Greystone Press.

Mueller, Tom
2013   *Extra Virginity: The Sublime and Scandalous World of Olive Oil.* W.W. Norton and Company.

Rodriguez, C.
2014   The Olive Oil Scam; If 80% is fake why do you keep buying it? Forbes Magazine Feb. 10 online, accessed June 18, 2018:
https://www.forbes.com/sites/ceciliarodriguez/2016/02/10/the-olive-oil-scam-if-80-is-fake-why-do-you-keep-buying-it/#79ce5c41639d

9. Pastoralism: Shepherding through the ages

Agnostic
2013   The spread of Christianity and the great civilizational fault line in Europe. *Face to Face Blog* Aug. 22, 2013. Accessed June 12, 2018:
http://akinokure.blogspot.ca/2013/08/the-spread-of-christianity-and-great.html

Alcorn, R.
2008   Shepherd Status. IN: *Come, Thou Long-Expected Jesus*, Nancy Guthrie (Editor) pp. 85-89. Wheaton, IL: Crossway Books.

Bailey, K.
2008   *Jesus through Middle Eastern Eyes; Cultural Studies in the Gospels.* Intervarsity Press, Downers Grove, IL.

Bignal, E. and D. McCracken
1996   Low-intensity farming systems in the conservation of the
        countryside. *Journal of Applied Ecology* 33, pp. 413-424.

Sarno, E.
2014   Historical maps and GIS environment as integrated methodology
        to rediscovery of cattle-track landscapes. a case study. *Review of
        historical geography and toponomastics* 17-18: 81-101.

UNESCO
n.d.   The Transhumance: The Royal Shepherd's Track. Accessed June
        12, 2018: http://whc.unesco.org/en/tentativelists/5005/

10. Tasting Landscape, Tasting the Past: A crash course in *terroir* and other sources of diversity

Trubek, A.
2008   *The Taste of Place: A Cultural Journey into Terroir*. Berkeley:
        University of California Press.

11. Cheese

Pollan, Michael
2013   *Cooked: A Natural History of Transformation*. London: Penguin.

12. Wine

Easton, S.
2012   *Primativo in Puglia*. Accessed May 9, 2016:
        http://www.winewisdom.com/articles/primitivo-in-puglia/

Gee, R.
2008   From corpse to ancestor. The role of tombside dining in the
        transformation of the body in ancient Rome. In: *The Materiality of
        Death. Bodies, Burials, Beliefs*, edited by F. Fahlander and T.
        Oestigaard, pp. 59-68. Oxford: Archaeopress.

Grout, J.
n.d.   *Wine and Rome*. Web page administered by the University of
        Chicago. Accessed May 9, 2016:
        http://penelope.uchicago.edu/~grout/encyclopaedia_romana/wine/wine

Marcis, R.
n.d.   *The Pleasurable Wines of Puglia.* Accessed May 9, 2016:
           http://www.winewordswisdom.com/wine_reviews/pleasurable-wines-of-
           puglia.html

McGovern, P.
2003   *Ancient Wine: The Search for the Origins of Viniculture.* Princeton:
           Princeton University Press.

no author
n.d.   *The wines of Puglia.* Accessed May 9, 2016:
           http://www.winesofpuglia.com/index.php/en/nero-di-troia

Polfer, M.
2000   Reconstructing funerary rituals: the evidence of ustrina and
           related archaeological structures. In: *Burial, Society, and Context in
           the Roman World,* edited by John Pearce, Martin Millet and
           Manuela Struck, pp. 30-44. Oxford: Oxbow Books.

Purcell, N.
1985   *Wine and Wealth in Ancient Italy.* Journal of Roman Studies Vol. 75:
           1-19.

Urwin, T.
1991   *Wine and the Vine: An Historical Geography of Viticulture and the Wine
           Trade.* Routledge, London.

13. The Amalfi Coast: The land where the lemon trees bloom

Aceto, S.
2015   Lemon Farmer in Amalfi. Personal communication during field
           research, 2015.

FAO
n.d.   Globally Important Agricultural Heritage Systems (GIAHS);
           Lemon Gardens, Southern Italy. Accessed May 10, 2017:
           http://www.fao.org/giahs/giahs-sites/europe-and-central-asia/lemon-gardens-
           southern-italy/en/

Fiorentino, G. et al.
n.d.   AGRUMED: The history of citrus fruits in the Mediterranean.
          Introductions, diversifications and uses. *Antiquity Online journal*,
          edited by Chris Scarre Durham University UK. Accessed May 20,
          1017 : http://antiquity.ac.uk/projgall/fiorentino339/

Grego, S.
n.d.   *Agricultural Heritage Systems: lemon gardens in southern Italy.* FAO
          document, accessed May 10, 2017:
          ftp://ftp.fao.org/sd/sda/GIAHS/italy_lemongardens_proposal_021007.pdf

Litchfield, R.
1997   "The Arab Invasions, and the Medieval Landscape of the
          "Mediterranean Garden." In: *History of the Italian Agricultural
          Landscape,* edited by Emilio Seren, pp. 72-73. Princeton: Princeton
          University Press.

Pagnoux, C. et al.
2012   The Introduction of Citrus in Italy with Reference to the
          Identification Problem of Seed Remains. *Vegetation history and
          Archaeobotany* 22: 421-38.

14. Lemons

Amalfi Lemon Experience
n.d.   Company website. Accessed June 12, 2018:
          https://amalfilemonexperience.it/

15. Of Nuns and Pastries: Cooking up traditions in God's kitchens

Brillat Savarin, J.A.
2011 (1825)   The Physiology of Taste: Or, Meditations on Transcendental
              Gastronomy. Translated and edited by M.F.K. Fisher. New
              York: Vintage Books.

Brumberg, J.
1988(1)   From Sainthood to Patienthood. In: *Fasting Girls: The
          Emergence of Anorexia Nervosa as a Modern Disease*, pp. 41-60.
          Harvard University Press, Cambridge MA.
1988(2)   The Appetite as Voice. In: *Fasting Girls: The Emergence of
          Anorexia Nervosa as a Modern Disease*, pp. 164-204. Cambridge
          MA: Harvard University Press

Di Schino, J.
1995   The Waning of Sexually Allusive Monastic Confectionary in Southern Italy. IN: *Disappearing Foods: Studies in Food and Dishes at Risk. Proceedings of the Oxford Symposium on Food and Cookery 1994*, edited by Harlan Walker, pp. 67-72. Blackawton: Prospect Books.

Dunbabin, T. J.
1948   *The Western Greeks. The History of Sicily and Southern Italy from the Foundation of the Greek Colonies to 480 BC.* Oxford: Clarendon Press.

Evangelisti, S.
2008   Nuns: A history of Convent Life 1450-1700. Oxford: Oxford University Press.

Mazzoni, C.
2005   How to Confect Convent Treats; Sweet Traditions and the Martyrdom of Saint Agatha. IN: *The Women in God's Kitchen; Cooking, Eating and Spiritual Writing*, pp. 74-86. New York: Continuum Press.

Newall, V.
1984   Easter Eggs: Symbols of Life and Renewal. *Folklore* 95(1): pp. 21-29.

Pasticceria Monastero Santa Chiara
n.d.   company website (in Italian). Accessed June 12, 2018: http://www.pasticceriamonasterosantachiara.it/

Poe, T.
2001   The Labour and Leisure of Food Production as a Mode of Ethnic Identity building Among Italians in Chicago, 1890-1940. *Rethinking History* 5(1): pp. 131-148.

Riley, G.
2007   *The Oxford Companion to Italian Food.* Oxford: Oxford University Press.

Salloum, H., M. Salloum and L. Salloum Elias
2013   Sweet Delights from a Thousand and One Nights: The Story of Traditional Arab Sweets. New York: I.B. Tauris and Co.

Scherb, M.
2009   *A Taste of Heaven: A Guide to Food and Drink Made by Monks and Nuns.* New York: Penguin Books.

Strocchia, S.
2009   *Nuns and Nunneries in Renaissance Florence.* Salt Lake City: John Hopkins University Press. Available online at https://muse.jhu.edu/books/9780801898624

Tarantino, M. and S. Terizani
2010   A Journey into the Imaginary of Sicilian Pastry. *Gastronomica* 10(3): pp. 45-51.
Villette, A.
2011   Nuns at Work. *Gastronomica*, 11(2): pp. 90-93.

Wright, C.
n.d.   *Cassata: The Sicilian Cake.* Accessed May 9, 2016: http://www.cliffordawright.com/caw/food/entries/display.php/topic_id/13/id/119/

16. Almonds

Bignal, E. and D. McCracken
1996   Low-Intensity Farming Systems in the Conservation of the Countryside. *Journal of Applied Ecology* Vol. 33, No. 3 (June 1996), pp. 413-424. DOI: 10.2307/2404973

Godini A.
2005   A Short History of Almond Cultivation in Apulia (southern Italy): Its Rise and Decline. IN: *XIII GREMPA Meeting on Almonds and Pistachios*, edited by M.M Oliveira and V. Cordeiro. pp. 207-214. Zaragoza: CIHEAM Options Méditerranéennes: Série A. Séminaires Méditerranéens; n. 63

Ladizinsky, G.
1999   On the Origin of Almonds. *Genetic Resources and Crop Evolution* 46 (2): 143–147.

Soyer, A.
2004 (1853)   Food, Cookery and Dining in Ancient Times. Reprinted by Dover Publications, Mineola NY.

Zohary, D., and M. Hopf
2000   *Domestication of plants in the old world: the origin and spread of cultivated plants in West Asia, Europe, and the Nile Valley.* Oxford: Oxford University Press.

17. Tradition Does Not Exist

Artisan Food Law
2013   Traditional Cheeses. Accessed June 10, 2017:
          http://www.artisanfoodlaw.co.uk/traditional-foods/dairy/dairy-cheese
2015   EU food hygiene rules – are they strangling small scale food production? Accessed June 12, 2018:
          http://www.artisanfoodlaw.co.uk/blog/traditional-foods/eu-food-hygiene-rules-%E2%80%93-are-they-strangling-small-scale-food-production
2016   Artisan cheese production – does hygiene policy help or hinder? Accessed June 12, 2018:
          http://www.artisanfoodlaw.co.uk/blog/traditional-foods/artisan-cheese-production-%E2%80%93-does-hygiene-policy-help-or-hinder

Food Standards Agency
n.d.   European Legislation and Enforcement. Accessed June 12, 2018:
          https://www.food.gov.uk/enforcement/regulation/europeleg

Toxey, A.
2004   Reinventing the Cave: Competing Images, Interpretations, and Representations of Matera, Italy. *Traditional Dwellings and Settlement Review* Volume 15(2): pp. 61-78. Accessed June 13, 2018:
          http://iaste.berkeley.edu/pdfs/15.2f-Spr04toxey-sml.pdf

18. Bread

19. Slow Food in a Fast World

de Tocqueville, A. (translated by H. Mansfield)
1835 (2002)   *Democracy in America.* Chicago: University of Chicago Press.

Dicke, J.
2008   *Delizia! The Epic History of the Italians and Their Food.* New York: Simon and Schuster.

Friedmann, H. and A. McNair
2008   Whose Rules Rule? Contested Projects to Certify 'Local Production for Distant Consumers'. *Journal of Agrarian Change*, Vol. 8, Nos. 2 and 3, April and July 2008: 408–434.

Ginsborg, P.
2003   A History of Contemporary Italy. New York: Palgrave Macmillan.

Meneley, A.
2004   Slow Food and Extra Virgin Olive Oil. *Anthropologica* 46: 165-176.

Montanari, M.
2012.   *Let the Meatballs Rest: And Other Stories About Food and Culture.* New York: Columbia University Press.

Petrini, C.
2007   *Slow Food Nation: Why Our Food Should Be Good, Clean, and Fair.* New York: Rizzoli ex Librus.

Sassatelli, R. and F. Davolio
2010   Consumption, Pleasure and Politics Slow Food and the Politico-aesthetic Problematization of Food. *Journal of Consumer Culture* 10(2): 202-232.

Schneider, S.
2008   Good, Clean, Fair: The Rhetoric of the Slow Food Movement. *College English*, Vol. 70, No. 4, Special Focus: Food (Mar., 2008): 384-402

References

INDEX

About the Author

Nicole Kilburn is an anthropologist at Camosun College in Victoria BC. She has a background in archaeology and has worked in Belize, the American Southwest, and British Columbia. Her interests in food anthropology have led to work in Italy and on indigenous food sovereignty projects in the Pacific Northwest. When she is not learning and teaching about how food connects people to their heritage and local landscapes, she may be found helping her husband cook great food for their two children and extended families and friends.

CPSIA information can be obtained
at www.ICGtesting.com
Printed in the USA
LVHW061557041218
598894LV00012B/17/P